Temperament and Child Psychopathology

About the series . . .

Series Editor: Alan E. Kazdin, Yale University

The Sage series in **Developmental Clinical Psychology and Psychiatry** is uniquely designed to serve several needs of the field. While the primary focus is on childhood psychopathology, the series also offers monographs prepared by experts in clinical child psychology, child psychiatry, child development, and related disciplines. The series draws upon multiple disciplines, as well as diverse views within a given discipline.

In this series...

Temperament and Child Psychopathology

William T. Garrison
Felton J. Earls

Volume 12.
Developmental Clinical Psychology and Psychiatry

SAGE PUBLICATIONS
The International Professional Publishers
Newbury Park   London   New Delhi

For Sean, Tanya, and Leigh

For information address:

SAGE Publications, Inc.
2111 West Hillcrest Drive
Newbury Park, California 91320

SAGE Publications Ltd.
28 Banner Street
London EC1Y 8QE
England

SAGE Publications India Pvt. Ltd.
M-32 Market
Greater Kailash I
New Delhi 110 048 India

Printed in the United States of America

Library of Congress Cataloging-in-Publication Data

Garrison, William T.
  Temperament and child psychopathology.

  (Developmental clinical psychology and psychiatry ;
v. 12)
  Bibliography: p.
  Includes indexes.
  1. Temperament in children.
2. Child psychopathology. I. Earls, Felton.
II. Title. III. Series. [DNLM: 1. Personality—
in infancy and childhood. 2. Psychopathology—
in infancy & childhood. W1 DE997NC v.12 /
WS 350 G242t]
RJ507.T45G37   1987   155.4   87-28388
ISBN 0-8039-2296-5

SECOND PRINTING, 1990

CONTENTS

SERIES EDITOR'S INTRODUCTION

Interest in child development and adjustment is by no means new. Yet only recently has the study of children benefited from advances in both clinical and scientific research. Advances in the social and biological sciences, the emergence of disciplines and subdisciplines that focus exclusively on childhood and adolescence, and greater appreciation of the impact of such influences as the family, peers, and school have helped accelerate research on developmental psychopathology. Apart from interest in the study of child development and adjustment for its own sake, the need to address clinical problems of adulthood naturally draws one to investigation to precursors in childhood and adolescence.

Within a relatively brief period, the study of psychopathology among children and adolescents has proliferated considerably. Several different professional journals, annual book series, and handbooks devoted entirely to the study of children and adolescents and their adjustment document the proliferation of work in the field. Nevertheless, there is a paucity of resource material that presents information in an authoritative, systematic, and disseminable fashion. There is a need within the field to convey the latest developments and to represent different disciplines, approaches, and conceptual views to the topics of childhood and adolescent adjustment and maladjustment.

The Sage Series in Developmental Clinical Psychology and Psychiatry is designed to serve uniquely several needs of the field. The series encompasses individual monographs prepared by experts in the fields of clinical child psychology, child psychiatry, child development, and related disciplines. The primary focus is on developmental psychopathology, which refers broadly here to the diagnosis, assessment, treatment, and prevention of problems that arise in the period from infancy through adolescence. A working assumption of the series is that understanding, identifying, and treating problems of youth must draw upon multiple disciplines and diverse views within a given discipline.

The task for individual contributors is to present the latest theory and research on various topics including specific types of dysfunction,

7

diagnostic and treatment approaches, and special problems areas that affect adjustment. Core topics within clinical work are addressed by the series. Authors are asked to bridge potential theory, research, and clinical practice, and to outline the current status and future directions. The goals of the series and the tasks presented to individual contributors are demanding. We have been extremely fortunate in recruiting leaders in the fields who have been able to translate their recognized scholarship and expertise into highly readable works on contemporary topics.

The present monograph, prepared by Drs. William T. Garrison and Felton J. Earls, is devoted to the topic of temperament and child psychopathology. The book discusses multifaceted research on child development and individual differences in relation to child functioning and psychopathology. Alternative views of temperament, the role of temperament in child development and child rearing are thoroughly traced. Several topics are carefully integrated including developmental continuities in the life span, genetic and psychosocial influence on development, and parent-child interaction. Classical longitudinal studies are presented and evaluated and their implications for theory and practice are developed. The book is unique in its breadth of coverage and remarkable balance in addressing research and practice and in raising substantive and methodological issues. The authors have conveyed the significance of temperament in the study of child functioning and the questions that wait to be addressed and have accomplished the task in a highly readable text.

—Alan E. Kazdin, Ph.D.

PREFACE

The concept of temperament is a controversial one from several vantage points. It goes against the grain of a powerful bias in empirical psychology, which depicts the environment as the primary influence in human behavior and personality. It also appears as an unwieldy and overly simplistic construct to those who seek adequately complex models to explain human nature and psychiatric etiologies. Critics from within and outside the areas of child development, psychiatry, and human biology have pointed out the theoretical and methodological shortcomings of the temperament literature. However, the study of temperament, or a concept like temperament, provides a focus that will eventually touch upon and influence multiple fields and perspectives pertinent to explanations of human nature. It is an idea that cannot be dismissed despite its inadequacies. If it could be, then we would have lost sight of it more than a thousand years ago. And yet the concept continues to stimulate theory and research.

By far the larger literature concerns temperament characteristics of children in the normal range of functioning. A much smaller group of studies exists that specifically looks at the relationship between temperament and child psychopathology. In order to be true to our goals in this volume we have attempted, wherever possible, to relate our review of major temperament approaches to the more narrow question of psychopathology. We have sought to provide historical and contemporary contexts for considering the associations among temperament dimensions and constructs in child psychopathology. At times we diverge from those approaches firmly situated in the temperament area and consider several research avenues that are pertinent to the broader issues. We have also attempted to place the knowledge and methods that the temperament literature provides within the context of clinical practice. Finally, the overview we provide for the reader is intended to lead to a consideration of those areas of research and theory that appear particularly promising in the future.

1

INTRODUCTION

Reflections on the nature of human personality can be found throughout recorded history. Notions about human nature personality in the mediations of both Eastern and Western philosophers and in the narratives of scores of writers and historians. They now provide a focus for the formal study of human behavior and development. It is important to point out that attention to early personality traits, or *temperament,* in children has been a relatively recent phenomenon as scientific interest in childhood for its own sake has evolved. This interest arises from several sources during the past century.

One could say that the history of childhood can be roughly divided into two eras. One that has occupied most of human history, and is still reflected in physical and psychological conditions in some parts of the globe, is oriented to survivorship and early initiation into adult responsibilities and labor. The second era was brought on by the industrial revolution. It conceives of a psychological dimension to childhood that has gradually over the past century overcome the economic importance of children. Theories concerning children prior to this relatively recent psychological phase thought of them as miniature adults. Once they survived the high mortality rate of infancy, they were nourished and protected for a few years and then assigned an increasing number of family and work responsibilities. Adolescence as a prolonged transitional period between childhood and adulthood was unknown throughout most of this history.

The reorganization of labor gradually relaxed the need to have children involved. Principles of universal education and theories of childhood innocence ushered in a more psychologically oriented phase in the history of childhood around the turn of the century. The concept of adolescence, the presumed deterministic nature of early childhood experience, and the measurement of intelligence represent advances that were rapidly and deeply inculcated into our social fabric. It is against this sociohistorical background that modern theories of temperament have developed.

Initially the child was studied to provide a reference point for understanding the origins of characteristics in adults. In Western philosophy, for example, various ideas put forth concerning human nature would often draw upon descriptions of the process through which moral, political, and intellectual character were formed during childhood. Few of these notions were truly developmental in approach, however. Attention to concepts we now categorize within temperament was limited in this tradition. Distinctions between people in regard to 'the passions' were typically made across *groups* of people, usually as a function of more superficial features such as race, class, or geographics. Here again, children themselves were of little interest, although some of our early notions concerning maturation and constitutional tendencies derive from theophilosophical traditions.

Later, as the child's status improved at a societal level, his or her personality would be viewed as manifesting *fluid* dimensions that *crystallized* or were made permanent as experience accrued. This particular perspective owes much of its popularity to a parallel course with the ascension of behaviorism and an emphasis on environmental influence in shaping all aspects of personality. This view is still present in modern theories of human personality and characterizes the approach of the DSM-III psychiatric taxonomy in its classification of personality disorders.

As the societal status and survivorship of children increased during the twentieth century, greater attention was paid to the health problems of the child. This focus on children provided the impetus for many of the studies we see today concerning child psychopathology, early human development, and the concept of *temperament*.

TOWARD A DEFINITION OF TEMPERAMENT

Various approaches to the concept of temperament have adopted somewhat different definitions of the term. It is useful at the outset to consider the range of such definitions. Each of the views described here will be treated in more detail in later chapters. The reader should be aware that recent articles summarizing the theoretical and measurement approaches to temperament are available elsewhere (Goldsmith et al.,

1987). We intend to provide only a brief synopsis to introduce some of the issues involved in the study of human temperament.

Adult personality theorists such as Cattell (1950) and Allport (1937) viewed temperament largely as hereditary characteristics that were somewhat resistant to environmental influence when compared to aspects of personality more determined through experiential factors. Allport emphasized the emotional or mood qualities that derive from temperament while Cattell discussed temperament largely in terms such as *impulsiveness* versus *reflectivity*, *threshold for excitability*, and so on.

Thomas and Chess (1977) are credited with developing an approach to temperament that eventually emphasized such traits as primarily manifest in the form of a *behavioral style*. By this they intend to view temperament as 'a general term referring to the *how* of behavior. It differs from ability, which is concerned with the *what* and *how well* of behaving, and from motivation, which accounts for *why* a person does what he is doing. Temperament by contrast concerns the *way* in which an individual behaves' (Thomas & Chess, 1977, p. 9). This definition of temperament underwent some alteration between the early sixties, when Thomas, Chess, and their colleagues first published on the subject, and the version they offer in the 1980s. This is detailed in Chapter 3 of this volume.

Another major definition of temperament seeks to emphasize the psychobiological bases of early behavioral traits (Rothbart & Derryberry, 1981). This approach examines the *reactive* aspects of infant behavior largely in terms of physiologic arousal, and the *active* qualities of self-regulation that implicate multiple dimensions such as cognition, perception, and affect. This definition or model of temperament also builds upon the basic tenet that temperament is constitutionally based and therefore measurable via physiologic indices and should be demonstrably constant across time and context.

Buss and Plomin (1975, 1984) also provide definitional guidance on the concept of temperament via a set of criteria that must be met. These criteria include evidence of a genetic component, stability during development, presence in adulthood, adaptive qualities, and presence in other animals. This definition derives directly from theoretical work by Allport (1937) and Diamond (1957) and essentially emphasizes the heritability and predictive value of temperament characteristics.

A more recent definition of temperament has been offered by Goldsmith and Campos (1982, p. 22) and employs *measurable behaviors in the infancy period* as its basis.

A *parameter of temperament* refers to the intensive or temporal characteristics of expression (e.g., latency to smile). An *expressive system for temperament* refers to any element of the behavioral repertoire which can function in the service of temperament (e.g., the facial expressive system, the motor system, or the vocal system). *Dimensions of temperament* refer to the content domains of individual differences which comprise temperament (e.g., fearfulness or irritability).

Each of the above definitions in modern research on temperament clearly derive from or are influenced by the particular instruments or operational approach of the investigators. This state of affairs has lead to some confusion for scholars who seek to offer an overview of the field of temperament research (Hubert, Wachs, Peters-Martin, & Gandour, 1982). It is also interesting to note that current temperament research has had little overlap with adult personality research, a large subtopical area in psychology. And finally, since we are considering definitions of temperament that provide the orientation for much of the empirical work, it is somewhat ironic that there is little connection between current research in developmental psychology and philosophy, a discipline that has had much to say about the nature of human beings.

RATIONALE FOR THE STUDY
OF HUMAN TEMPERAMENT

It is also useful at the outset to consider the reasons we choose to study a concept like temperament. The essential rationale involves both intellectual curiosity about the origins of human behavior and pragmatic concerns arising from public health issues. The impetus for the modern study of temperament derives from a longstanding philosophical tradition of inquiry into the nature of persons, as well as from more recent initiatives to understand the etiology of mental health disorders and psychological coping. The main questions in both the philosophical and psychological literatures on temperament, or early personality traits, have been the following:

(1) To what degree do biologic factors influence the course of human development? Some writers and researchers have chosen to focus on genetic variables versus constitutional variables (which may not be heritable) but the presumption in each is that biologic substrates influence behavior and personality to some extent.

(2) How are biologic factors affected by the environment? Most modern researchers in the area of temperament are now interested in the process

whereby continuity and discontinuity in behavior are created. All major theoretical and methodological approaches in this area acknowledge that environmental forces shape human behavior and personality. Despite the wide acceptance of the notion that some form of interaction between constitutional traits and experience renders human behavior, inquiry into this area is compelled by a desire to know the primacy of nature in the unfolding of personal life history.

Workers in the area of temperament research will point to many interrelated goals and rationales for their studies. These include description of normal and abnormal behavioral development in same- and cross-cultural contexts, estimation of genetic influence on behavior, and clinical applications of temperament concepts/methods for specific human problems such as child psychopathology and the problems of normal development.

TEMPERAMENT AND CHILD PSYCHOPATHOLOGY

The relationship between concepts about human temperament on the one hand, and concepts of child psychopathology on the other, presents a host of problematic issues. First of all, it must be recognized that empirical studies relevant to both concepts are relatively few and critical obstacles have yet to be overcome. We must remember that empirical work on the nature of intelligence, a more established area of child development research, is only about 80 years old. Even in that realm much remains to be known about origins. Empirical research on temperament is less than 25 years old and basic methodological work remains to be done prior to extensive speculation concerning its nature, course, or relationship with psychological disorder. Both areas, while thought to be rather distinct by some, have considerable overlap in both theoretical and methodologic approaches. We will see, for example, that many of the dimensions identified as temperamentally based are also used in the language of clinical diagnosis with children. Similarly, some of the theoretical speculation about the process of temperament in terms of physiological response and activation (for example, arousal or attention) does not seem very removed from some clinical explanations for the etiology of disorder (for example, anxiety or cognitive distractibility).

Both are stuck on some basic problems with definition that hinder cohesion and consensus across studies and also impede progress in etiologic inquiry. Despite these considerable problems, multiple models of both temperament and psychopathology are available. Temperament, or biologic input, is a variable included in most formal and informal theories of human nature and behavior. Some have viewed this factor as primary in the development of certain psychiatric disorders. Others have included it within models that afford environmental experience primary influence. The most popular current view of psychopathology would probably not hazard to stipulate which plays a more important role, choosing instead to emphasize a complex interaction of multiple variables. Since the notion of biologic influence is central to many perspectives on early personality development and the course of mental illness, it is natural that this wedding of concepts has occurred. In the specific approaches that seek to relate temperament characteristics and child behavior problems, however, some distinctions in both conceptual and methodological areas have yet to be made in a clear fashion.

Despite these important problems, an interesting and useful literature on temperament and child psychopathology now exists. The value of this body of research may reside more in the vocabulary and techniques it offers than in any clarification concerning process or etiology. In the following chapters we will discuss, in a rather selective manner, some of the origins of temperament notions. We will also consider the methods and theories that characterize the modern study of temperament through review of major studies. Then we will specifically examine the empirical literature on the relationship between temperament and child psychopathology. As a follow-up to that discussion we will draw upon several broad dimensions of child behavior and dysfunction as the context for a consideration of clinical issues relevant to applications of temperament theory and methods. Finally, we will attempt to summarize the major points of the volume and offer a critique of the area that may help to point the way to promising avenues of inquiry.

2

PERSPECTIVES ON TEMPERAMENT

ANCIENT THEORIES

Imagine that the whole range of human personality could be reduced to four prototypes: the *melancholic*, the *choleric*, the *phlegmatic*, and the *sanguine*. Each has a unique physiological basis caused by the influence of four *humors: black bile* (or congealed blood), *yellow bile, phlegm,* and *blood.* This was the theory of Galen, the great Roman physician who lived in the second century, A.D. His theory represented a culmination of observational studies that probably began thousands of years before him. Galen dissected the Barbary ape, a revolutionary pursuit for his time, and reasoned from this the role of the humors in personality, health, and illness. His studies led him to the belief that the liver was the seat of the soul and the primary organ of the body. Through his experiments, teachings, and writing he became one of the founding fathers of medicine. His theories and the system of therapeutics on which it was based remained the predominant influence in medicine for at least 1400 years.

Health was conceived of as an equilibrium of the four humors. The task of therapeutics was to reestablish this equilibrium so as to restore health in an ill person. The physician was given clues as to the nature of the patient's illness by paying close attention to personality traits. A morose, pessimistic person had an excess of black bile. One who was ambitious, shrewd, revengeful, proud, lean, and quick to anger had an excess of yellow bile. The phlegmatic person was stolid, apathetic, and undemonstrative, while the sanguine person was optimistic, enthusiastic, and excitable. Though Galen's influence did eventually yield to the renaissance of medicine that began in the sixteenth century, the concept of the four temperaments, or the four *complexions*, as they were also known, have made a deep impression on our concepts of personality. They are useful adjectives in the language of describing personal qualities even today.

While Galen's contribution is a landmark in the recorded history of Western civilization, theories about personality are known to have been formulated in ancient India and China thousands of years prior to him. It seems that one of the early tasks of civilization was to devise a means of accounting for individual differences between persons and to relate such differences to health practices. The ancient Hindus formulated a system in which an orderly relationship existed between aspects of the natural environment and personality. *Air, water,* and *geographic location* influenced the three elementary substances of the body: the *spirit,* seated below the navel; *phlegm,* seated above the heart; and bile, located between the zones of phlegm and spirit. Unlike Galen's theory, which positioned a balance between the humors as the mechanism of health and disease, this theory was concerned with the balance between environment and body. Moving to a new environment might be the way to restore health. The purpose of therapeutics was to analyze the composition of places in relationship to disease.

Traditional Chinese medicine offers another version on a somewhat similar theme. In this theory human nature is composed of two forces or spirits: *yin,* which is dark, female, and identified with the earth, and *yang,* which is active, light, and represented by the heavens. These forces combined to determine one's character and one's health. They also regulate the flow of fluids that exist in channels throughout the body. Acupuncture was developed as a therapeutic technique to influence the flow of these fluids.

The theories formulated by the ancient Hindus and Chinese probably influenced Hippocrates and other Greek physicians and philosophers, for there too we find notions of one's habitat influencing bodily functions and aspects of the humors or fluids. Thus Galen's ideas, which seem so primitive to us now, represented a culmination of reflections for his time on the relationship of temperament to health that existed from the beginning of civilization.

Though somewhat remote, these notions are intriguing for several reasons. First, they all represent efforts to understand behavior through physiology. In that sense they are distinguished from occult or purely spiritualist theories, some of which have survived despite efforts to establish a rational basis for medical practices. Second, they tended to be holistic, conceiving of mind, body, and spirit as a sum. Third, they were used as a basis for medical therapeutics. It is precisely in these connections that the quest for an understanding of personality remains unresolved. The effort to formulate temperament or personality in physiologic terms, just in the past century, has progressed from considerations on the configuration of the cranium to constitutional types, to variations in the structure of the nervous system, and, most recently, to genetics. It would not be preposterous to say that in the past 4000 years we have gone from fluids to humors, to neurons, and now to genes in an effort to comprehend differences in human temperament. The success of this endeavor has not really attracted wide public attention. Astrology is still more popular than any scientific theory of personality.

PSYCHOLOGICAL VIEWS

The study of the mental qualities and the behavior of humans became a scientific pursuit during the latter part of the nineteenth century. Immediately preceding this, for 300 years, tremendous progress had been made in revising the concepts of medicine and physiology that had been derived from the Greeks and Romans. Dissection of cadavers had revealed that the brain, not the liver, was the organ of the senses and behavior. Blood, not bile, was the essential constituent of organ functioning. The inspiration that gave birth to psychology was the desire to document the principles and physiological bases of behavior. For the past century the efforts to achieve this understanding have been pursued enthusiastically. The highlights of these contributions include the work of Pavlov (1927), Freud (1950), and Eysenck and Eysenck (1969). Other notable contributions have been made by Sheldon (1942), Sjobring (1973), Allport (1961), Cattell (1950), and Guilford (1959), among others. It is beyond the scope of this book to review the contributions of these scientists. In fact, the topic of personality is so fundamental to psychology that the literature on the subject is truly voluminous. The purpose here is to extract from this body of knowledge and theory those concepts that bear on the focused interest in how temperamental differences in children may be related to a vulnerability or susceptibility to develop a psychiatric disorder.

To accomplish this the various approaches have all struggled with a similar set of problems. The first is to develop an adequate system of classification. The second is to formulate a mechanism or a set of mechanisms that relate temperament to physiology. The third is to test the theory through scientific experiments or therapeutic interventions. The particular ways in which scientists approach these tasks reflects differences in emphasis. These are instructive since a quick review indicates various difficulties that have confronted each investigator attempting to place a personality theory on a solid base of empiricism and experimental evidence. An examination of a few of the greatest psychologists of our era will make the point.

Pavlov, a psychologist whose work greatly influenced experimental psychology, proposed that humans had different types of nervous systems: *Type A* was relatively easy to train and *Type B* was more resistant to training in his conditioning experiments. The implications of this distinction are of great importance because they suggest that differences in learning may be a fundamental property of the nervous system. Russian psychologists incorporated Pavlov's theory into their work. Pavlov's ideas continue to have an important place in efforts to locate a physiological basis to learning and a therapeutic application of temperament. Pavlov's influence in the United States is reflected primarily in the work of Watson (1924), Skinner, and other behaviorists, who have tended to dismiss this typology and disregard the importance of innate or physiological differences in the nervous system. Thus the therapeutic applications of behavior modification and biofeedback, which are derived from behaviorism, tend to minimize individual differences in judging the response to treatment.

Freud's theory of psychoanalysis has gained a more central place in Western psychological theories than has Pavlov's. It is an elaborate theory and is particularly compelling in that it formulates detailed psychological mechanisms that give rise to psychopathology. Although in his time Freud had relatively advanced ideas about the role of the nervous system in human behavior, he believed that an understanding of mind was an important first step in learning how nervous activity influenced behavior. Throughout his life he sought to identify and describe mental phenomena with little opportunity to return to his earlier speculations on how these phenomena might be related to the nervous system. His original belief, however, that psychoanalysis would ultimately be founded on principles of neurophysiology has never lost its luster.

In regard to personality, Freud's contribution was to propose a developmental-experiential dimension. *Oral, anal, phallic,* and *genital* character traits were developmentally acquired. Each represented a stage in the psychological growth of a child from infancy to middle childhood. At each stage particular personality traits came to dominate the child; the means through which this occurred was never fully explained. Depending on the child's environment, he or she either successfully negotiated through these five hierarchically arranged stages or stagnated. Personality was shaped by the passage or its failure of passage through these stages. Only a vague aspect of the theory articulates a physiological basis for this developmental progression. Conceptually, the implications carried by these abstract developmental stages are distinctly foreign from the notion of innately derived, physiologically controlled temperament. It is in this sense that the evolution of psychoanalysis remains incomplete and, in several respects, disconfirmable as theory. Freud's elegant theory has become remote to scientific skepticism and thus has failed to capture the imagination of recent generations of empirically oriented investigators.

An equally compelling but much less well known theory of personality was formulated by Sjobring (1973), a Swedish psychiatrist. He postulates that there are four dimensions of personality: *capacity, validity, stability,* and *solidity.* Capacity is the genetic substrate for intelligence; Validity is the degree of energy available for central nervous system functioning; Stability is the maximum potential in nervous activity that can be achieved by a person; and Solidity is the extent to which this potential must be replenished by experience to maintain its maximum level. The various types that are derived from these traits are displayed in Tables 2.1 and 2.2. The details of this particular theory are included since they are representative of other major theories of personality in approach. What is compelling about Sjobring's ideas is that the traits go beyond description to connote functional dimensions of personality as well. Implicit in the conceptualization of these personality constructs are both genetic and physiologic aspects of the nervous system. These dynamic elements are then combined to characterize personality. Sjobring's theory is an elaboration on the Pavlovian model in which personality traits are viewed as manifestations of a neurobiological substrate. To be consistent with current ways of viewing temperament in children, a psychological theory of adult personality will need to include these notions.

TABLE 2.1

Sjobring Personality Constructs

Capacity:	genetic substrate for intellectual development.
Validity:	degree of energy available for nervous system functioning.
Stability:	maximum potential achievable given the person's nervous substrate.
Solidity:	the extent to which this potential must be replenished by experience to maintain its maximum level.

The Pavlovian, Freudian, and Sjobringian approaches serve as foundations for a physiological-developmental theory for personality, and for therapeutics applied to illnesses influenced by personality as well as personality disorders. They have been supplemented by a number of theories that have formulated personality typologies. For example, Sheldon (1942) proposed a relationship between body build and personality. Eysenck (1969), using a factor-analytic approach to describe personality traits, proposed a two-dimensional system contrasting neurotic and psychotic styles. A typology based on discrete classes, as in the body-build hypothesis, is different in implication from one based on variation across dimensions. A dimensional theory would suggest that each individual has some degree of the trait being measured. Eysenck's theory represents an important contribution in that it measures two fundamental characteristics of personality that are hypothesized to exist in all persons along such a dimension.

GENETIC AND NEUROBIOLOGICAL DETERMINANTS

Let us now consider theoretical views on the nature of the relationship between genes and behavior. Genes are a set of rules for specifying and maintaining bodily structures. Because the interest here is in studying behavior as it is manifested in various temperamental characteristics, the body structures of concern are in the brain. But what is known about how genes influence behavior? More precisely, how do genes determine brain structures and functions that in turn determine what may be termed temperamental or constitutionally based qualities ?

In thinking about the relationships between genes, the brain, and behavior, it is important to have a basic understanding of what behavior

TABLE 2.2
Sjobring's Eight Pure Types

Subcapable:	Inadaptable, crude and lacking in nuances, shortsighted and restricted, coarse, blunt, hasty and impulsive, obtuse and torpid in thought
Supercapable:	Sensitive, subtle, talented, adaptable, possessed of breadth and depth of view, deliberate and reflective, quick, keen, and understanding
Subvalid:	Cautious and uncertain, reserved, precise, industrious, scrupulous, habit-bound and narrow in perspective, prone to tension and fatigue, possessed of a need to be busy, circumscribed and vulnerable
Supervalid:	Venturesome, active, persevering, alert, confident, prepared and enterprising, broad in perspective, calm and efficient, independent
Substable:	Warm, hearty, clumsy, naive, maladroit and heavy moving, concrete in thought, interested in people, poorly integrated and intuitive
Superstable:	Cool, detached, and steady in mood, clever, abstract in thought, sophisticated, elegant, adroit and agile, interested in ideas and reflective, fixed in habits and a lover of one's ease
Subsolid:	Mobile and flexible, fragmented and loose, personal and egocentric, unpredictable, subjective, impulsive, actor and charmer
Supersolid:	Slow and steady, earnest, dependable, objective, circumspect, judicious, rigid and inflexible, dry, objective and realistic, harsh and self-sufficient, consistent and firm of purpose

is. Behavior is goal-directed activity in which the fundamental purposes are survival and procreation. This basic principle of evolutionary biology applies to all animals. Humans have evolved to a point at which the purposes of behavior have become extraordinarily complex. Even apparently simple behaviors serving the most basic biologic functions of food gathering and mating can involve elaborate and obscure (to the observer) activities. Behavior that is more complex than this, for example, those involved with political or artistic activities, is practically beyond the imagination of scientists interested in the relationship of brain to behavior.

It is this evolved capacity for complex behavior that created the idea of a *mind*. For hundreds of years philosophers and scientists have debated *dualism* versus *monism*. Dualism, most formally developed by

Descartes and Leibniz, claims that the mind operates on a set of laws that are distinct from those governing the activities of the brain. The mind has a unique existence of its own, even if it is dependent—in a material sense only—on the brain. Monists, on the other hand, argue that the mind is just an expression of the brain. Mind emanates from nervous tissue in a way that makes them inextricable.

In the last quarter-century neurobiology has grown at an exponential rate. It is now possible to envision how the brain determines thinking, mood, and motivation; and how these mental qualities in turn regulate behavior. Science is on the horizon of understanding how genes regulate the development of nervous structures. Perhaps in ten to twenty years it will be possible to state lawful relationships between genes and brain structures, and between certain demarcated brain structures and behavior. In all likelihood these will not be based on the types of mechanisms and processes that conform to the laws of physics and chemistry, but dynamic, open, and highly flexible processes. Viewed from the current perspective of developmental neurobiological research, it will probably be the case that as rules for specifying brain structures are delineated, we will understand how these structural and functional elements determine personality characteristics. It is against this rapidly growing scientific background that the issue of genetic influences on temperament must be evaluated.

Sex Chromosomes and Temperament

The most obvious way to begin examining genetic influences on behavior is to study sex differences. The presence at chromosome 46 of the XY pattern in the human male and an XX pattern in the female represent a potential source for behavioral differences. This issue has been studied in two ways: first, by directly examining various types of behaviors, normal and abnormal, between the sexes; and second, by studying various aberrations in the pattern of sex chromosomes, such as the XO pattern in Turner's syndrome, the XXY in Klinefelter's Syndrome, and the XYY pattern behavioral signs.

Research has suggested that males are more active and exhibit more aggressive behavior than girls. Alternatively, girls have been described as more socially attuned than boys (Maccoby & Jacklin, 1974). These generalizations from the research literature have been borne out in the data from our own longitudinal studies of very young children (Earls,

1980; Garrison & Earls, 1983). On seven of the nine temperament dimensions hypothesized by Thomas and Chess (see Chapter 3) there were no apparent differences among very young children as a function of sex. These results are generally consistent with other studies. On observing children in a free play situation, however, striking differences in the selection and use of toys did occur. Boys tended to select transportation items, while girls preferred household objects. Of the many types of toys selected, boys were much more likely to employ them as projectiles or as weapons, while girls would engage in caretaking behavior and less aggressive fantasy play. These types of differences were interpreted to reflect more the acquired interests of boys and girls rather than differences in gender-mediated temperament. However, the fact that they are present so early in development and appear to be stereotyped raises an important question regarding the origins of eventual sex differences in behavior.

Could the predispositions for the sex differences revealed in play be innately derived? Why would such a dramatic difference be seen in symbolic play when, viewed from the results on measuring temperament, differences between the sexes are not so large? The answer to the first question is affirmative. Under direction of the Y chromosome the testes begin to secrete testosterone toward the end of the first trimester of gestation. This continues throughout development reaching a peak late in the gestational period and again at puberty. Evidence exists that testosterone has a direct influence on nervous structures, particularly the area of the preoptic nucleus of the hypothalamus. What is most interesting about these developmental events is that there is no established counterpart to the male pattern. It is as if the basic plan is to produce a female.

Although parts of the puzzle will need to be filled out in more detail, it is conceivable that a set of instructions emanate from the Y chromosome to produce testosterone, which in turn creates structural differences in the nervous system. These structures are probably a necessary condition for the appearance of observed differences in the behavior of males and females.

A number of aberrations occur in the configuration of sex chromosomes that permit an extension of observations derived from normal development. One configuration is characterized by the presence of more than one Y chromosome. It is believed that this configuration should create an exaggeration of the male pattern of behavior. Actual observation of boys with this pattern has failed to confirm this hypothesis, although there is some evidence to support increased likelihood for violent behavior in male criminals with 46-XYY karyotype. Another pattern, known as Klinefelter's Syndrome, is manifested by the XXY configuration. In this case the predicted observation would be that the presence of the second X chromosome would suppress masculine behavior. Actual evidence lends only modest support to this hypothesis. In Turner's Syndrome, in which an XO pattern is present, feminine behavior is present despite the abnormalities in the reproductive system.

Another experiment of nature that potentially may help reveal more about the innate basis of behavioral differences between the sexes is the syndrome of congenital adrenal hyperplasia. In this disorder a metabolic error occurs in the production of hydrocortisone, the chief hormone of the adrenal cortex. An enzymatic defect results in the accumulation of androgens, which prematurely virilize the male and produce a syndrome of pseudohermaphroditism in the female. The enlargement of the clitoris that accompanies fetal exposure to high levels of androgens can lead to incorrect assignment of sex. In some cases girls with this disorder have accidentally been raised as boys for various lengths of time before the correct diagnosis is made. Naturally, this creates quite a complex and difficult decision regarding how late in development sex identity can be changed. With increased recognition of the disorder and improved diagnostic methods, the correct diagnosis is now being made at birth. This makes it possible to examine the prenatal effect of androgens on the brain without the bias of sex-specific socialization practices. Results on the behavior and interests of girls with this syndrome at birth are not yet available.

Autosomal Chromosomes and Temperament

This brief review of some of the ways in which biologically determined sex differences may result in stereotypical behavioral differences is one approach to demonstrating the influence of genetics on temperament. In the study of psychopathology a frequent question is whether a given disorder is X-linked or Y-linked. Despite clear sex differences in the prevalence and incidence of several types of psychiatric disorders (for example, alcoholism and antisocial personality disorder predominate in males; depression and anxiety predominate in females) none have been shown so far to be linked to the X or Y chromosome. An exciting and important research activity is currently under way in which efforts to associate various psychiatric disorders with specific locations on the genome (Cloninger, Reich, & Yokoyama, 1983). It is unlikely that a psychiatric disorder represents a phenotype. This is primarily because by definition psychiatric disorders represent a combination of features. Most disorders are heterogeneous in nature: Different combinations of symptoms of a syndrome make up distinct subtypes. Because of this the search for the phenotype must involve physiological and behavioral measures that may represent a vulnerability common to all the subtypes of a disorder. It is in this connection that the study of temperament is most important. Thus in examining the possible linkage between the genome and psychopathology, it may be most useful to couch the question in terms of genetic determinants of temperament. Very few data exist to examine this question in detail. Perhaps the best studied condition is Down's Syndrome, in which the observation has been repeatedly made that children affected with this syndrome have an easy, docile, and sociable temperament. The chromosomal defect in Down's Syndrome, known as 21 trisomy, produces a number of structural abnormalities (involving the heart and facial configuration) and mental retardation (which is probably related to a structural abnormality of the brain). It seems likely that the temperament associated with the syndrome is determined by the same chromosomal defect responsible for other structural abnormalities but, of course, this has not been demonstrated. The consequence of this type of temperament appears to be to protect the retarded child from parental neglect or rejection. It could be surmised that children and adults with Down's Syndrome would have lower prevalence of psychiatric disorder than other retarded individuals because of their easy temperaments (Gunn & Berry, 1985).

Little is known about possible linkages between genes, chromosomes, and behavioral phenotypes. However, there are important clues that certain types of psychiatric problems may be connected with specific chromosomes (Cloninger et al., 1983).

**Possible Genetic
Determinants of Personality**

Family, twin, and adoption study designs have been used to examine genetic influences on temperament and personality. In family studies the strength of correlation between personality features of parents and children is examined. In twin studies a comparison of monozygotic and dizygotic pairs is made. In adoption studies comparisons are made between biologically related individuals reared apart. Of these various designs twin studies have been by far the most prevalent. What has been most attractive about the twin study design is that it makes longitudinal studies from birth feasible. Over the past two decades several major longitudinal studies have been carried out, the interim results of which have been carefully reviewed elsewhere (Goldsmith, 1983). They consistently show that some types of temperament traits have a higher correlation in monozygotic (MZ) as compared to dizygotic (DZ) twins. *Activity level* and *social introversion-extroversion* show the higher heritability based on these studies, while *aggression* and *fearfulness* produce much weaker evidence of genetic influence. As these studies track the stability and change of early identified traits, the size of the MZ/DZ difference shrinks, although identical twins tend to remain more alike than fraternal twins. These studies have struggled with a number of serious limitations, such as inadequate sample size, possible biases in parent ratings and self-report measures, and failure to take into account the effects of nonrandom mating. However, they combine to produce a considerable body of evidence in support of the heritability of temperament. Given our knowledge of neurobiology, it is not surprising that behavior is under the influence of brain structures and activities that are genetically influenced. It would be helpful to know to what extent specific temperament traits were heritable. Identification of such traits early in development might then serve child-rearing or clinical purposes, if indeed they were known to be shaped primarily by genetics versus environmental experience.

The issue of innate determinants of personality has also been examined—though rather superficially—from the perspective of population genetics. Two types of comparison have been made. Black infants have been reported to have a relative advance in motor development, which may underlie differences in activity level and physical skill development. Although this was assumed to be a genetically determined difference between Black and Caucasian infants, it has been pointed out that the high demand for physical labor of African women, in particular, may be the cause of such advanced motor development in their infants (Super, 1976). Similarly, Japanese infants have been described as less reactive to physical and social stimuli than Caucasian infants. Again the issue of genetic versus child-rearing practices must be considered. These types of studies point out the great difficulty in studying personality from a population perspective. Perhaps the inherent difficulty of these types of studies, given their benefit to society, contributes to their being fairly unpopular. Further, it should be pointed out that although these studies are relevant to issues of population genetics, the design of large-scale projects to examine within- and between-population differences in temperament has not yet begun.

This discussion of genetic influences in temperament serves to point out a two-step process. The first step involves the nature of genetic control over areas of the central nervous system that governs behavior. The second step involves understanding the mechanism by which the properties of the nervous system regulate the particular behaviors that are subsumed by the definition of temperament. This regulatory process must be assumed to be influenced by the physical (for example, nutrition) and social (for example, parental bonding), but the processes through which this occurs are still poorly understood.

SUMMARY

This chapter began by reviewing the speculations that philosophers, physicians, and, more recently, psychologists have had about the nature of human personality over thousands of years. Much of this effort has been directed toward uncovering a physiological basis for understanding differences in human temperaments. This striving seems most conscientiously motivated by the hope that understanding the origins of individual differences in personality may aid physicians, psychologists, and other professionals working to improve the mental health of human groups in some substantial way.

With the emergence of the science of psychology and increased attention to the uniqueness of children in this century, the concept of personality differences has been solidly placed within a developmental perspective. It has been in this context that the search for a physiological or material basis for personality has intensified. Many of the greatest psychologists of this century have occupied themselves with the task of devising classificatory schemes that allow one to measure and interpret human differences in a functional manner. These efforts have been followed by the work of developmentalists who believe that temperament may have genetic and biologic origins. To examine this hypothesis broadly requires contributions from a number of areas and a variety of approaches. Individuals with specific medical syndromes have been examined in an effort to correlate constitutional aberrations and personality traits that may derive from known chromosomal or genetic defects. Down's Syndrome is perhaps the best studied example. Other approaches have involved the use of twin studies to examine personality characteristics of individuals who share endowments derived from the same genes. Finally, adoption studies have been used in an effort to separate genetic influences obtained from biological parents from environmental influences, which can be traced to adoptive parents.

All these efforts have been useful in providing support to the general hypothesis that genes determine personality differences to some degree. But, as with the ancient physicians, this conclusion is based on passive observations. The mass of data coming from these studies fails to disconfirm the genetic hypothesis, but researchers are not in a position to confirm it since that requires experimentation and manipulation. Though it may seem farfetched, given the rapidity with which the human genome is currently being mapped, it is possible that one day parents will be given a read out of the genetic composition of their children at birth (or prenatally). Once science has developed to that point, however, human experimentation with genes that control behavior and contribute to personality may indeed be feasible.

Even if this were possible, its desirability would have to be challenged for at least two major reasons. The relationship between genotype and phenotype of behavior is not understood. As Scarr and McCartney (1983) suggest, the relationship may be primarily unidirectional, with the individual having a large role in selecting features of the environment on which to thrive. On the other hand, the extraordinary immaturity of human infants, relative to other mammalian species, suggests an important and prolonged role of the environment in shaping and tuning personality. In this scenario, genes may serve the role of sustaining certain basic neural functions, but the psychological elements that compose personality may be represented on an entirely different level of organization. They may be regulated more by the social environment than by physiological mechanisms in the brain.

The second problem looms much larger and concerns the functions of human diversity. Evolutionary biology instructs us that establishing and maintaining diverse characteristics contributes to the adaptability and robustness of a species. It certainly seems justifiable to regard humans as having achieved some success thus far in evolution. Much of the success is based on our industry and capacity to create complex social institutions. No doubt the presence of diverse personality traits has contributed fundamentally to these aspects of our achievement. What we have not achieved, either philosophically or scientifically, is an understanding of what role individual differences in behavior contribute to the inclusive fitness of the species (Buss, 1984). It seems necessary to have established a framework of understanding why we are different before we can permit the science of genetics, no matter how technologically advanced, to work at redesigning human characteristics. For the foreseeable future, if it is to be allowed at all, genetic engineering should be directed toward alleviating human suffering in carefully diagnosed individuals. It seems along this path that the study of the genetics of temperament and its possible links to psychopathology is most clearly justifiable.

3

THEORY AND METHODS
IN THE STUDY
OF TEMPERAMENT

CONTEMPORARY THEORIES OF TEMPERAMENT

The burgeoning interest in temperament has been evidenced by a recent increase in both empirical studies and theoretical work on the topic. It can be argued that the scientific study of temperament has really only begun, but the controversy that characterizes this field has origins in a long-standing debate in psychology, philosophy, and human biology. This debate involves the definition, life course, and practical significance of individual differences. The most recent wave of investigators on the topic of temperament has been composed of persons coming from several different professional disciplines, among them psychiatry, psychology, genetics, anthropology, and pediatrics. As a result, valuable perspectives have been introduced to the study of temperament in the past quarter-century and proponents of each are involved in an active and constructive dialogue.

This chapter highlights the issues involved in defining what temperament is and how it might be manifested (that is, how we might observe and measure it) across the infancy through childhood years. We will see here that various approaches to measuring individual differences in children have been duly determined by the theoretical underpinnings of each investigator's inquiry. Also, we find in this chapter that two interrelated questions inevitably arise when conclusions across methods and findings are attempted. First, the issue of the *continuity* versus *discontinuity of temperament* is at the core of various definitions of the construct. Second, the degree to which temperament is something *within the child* versus something *between the child and others* also emerges as a critical concern. We hope that this discussion of the current state of the art in temperament research and theory will equip the reader for even thornier issues in Chapter 4, where we consider the purported relationship between temperament characteristics and the development of psychopathology during childhood.

Major Theories of Temperament

The work of Alexander Thomas, Stella Chess, and their associates at New York University Medical Center has served to fuel the resurgence of interest in the study of individual differences during infancy and early childhood. Their studies from the New York Longitudinal Survey (NYLS) have generated interesting possibilities for the study of early human development and have also set the tone of much of the subsequent work in this area (Thomas & Chess, 1968, 1977, 1984; Thomas, Chess, Birch, Hertzig, & Korn, 1963).

Relying heavily upon the reports of 141 mothers with infants, Thomas and Chess sought to construct a multidimensional description of early *behavioral style.* Their initial theoretical perspective appeared to emphasize the organismic contribution of genetic and physiological factors over environmental variables such as early social interaction. As the NYLS progressed, however, hypotheses concerning the concept of temperament became more *interactional,* that is, emphasis was placed upon temperament as a phenomenon largely created through transactions between the child and his or her environment. Despite this, an emphasis on characteristics in the child that have an organismic origin can be found in most of the work Thomas and Chess have produced. It is important to realize that this perspective during the late sixties and early seventies was generally at odds with popular conceptions depicting the environment (that is, the mother) as the primary influence during early child development. Also, in our discussions here we must remember that Thomas and Chess were most interested in identifying dimensions of individual difference that could be related to the subsequent development of psychopathology and behavior disorders in these children. Their findings will be addressed further in Chapter 4.

For the purposes of the present discussion, a consideration of the basic findings regarding the stability of temperament dimensions is most relevant. Thomas and his associates offered nine separate dimensions of temperament derived from an *inductive content analysis* of parental descriptions of infant behavior from the NYLS sample. These nine categories and their definitions are presented in Table 3.1. More than one critic through the years has found the methodology reported by Thomas and his colleagues to be a bit unclear and not conducive to replication attempts.

Through factor-analytic methods Thomas and colleagues identified three general constellations of temperament based upon combinations of more than one dimension. They reported that roughly 40% of their sample could be described as *EASY* children. By this they implied that such infants were viewed as high in *rhythmicity* (regular sleep and feeding schedules), high in *adaptability* (could accept changes in the environment easily and quickly), and not overly *active, intense,* or *moody.* Another group of children, about 15% of their original sample, were labeled as *SLOW-TO-WARM-UP.* These children combined slower adaptability to new situations with mildly intense and negative responsivity. Over time and repeated exposure, however, these children would adapt positively with 'interest and involvement' (Thomas & Chess, 1977, p. 23). About 10% of the NYLS sample fell into a category labeled *DIFFICULT* child. Thomas and Chess succinctly characterize this child for us:

> Irregularity in biological functions, negative withdrawal responses to new stimuli, nonadaptability or slow adaptability to change, and intense mood expression which are frequently negative. These children show irregular sleep and feeding schedules, slow acceptance of new foods, prolonged adjustment periods to new routines, people, or situations, and relatively frequent and loud periods of crying. Laughter, also, is characteristically loud. Frustration typically produces a violent tantrum. (Thomas & Chess, 1977: p. 23)

Briefly stated, Thomas and Chess viewed these nine dimensions, and their combinations, as useful concepts for describing the behavioral style of the infant or young child. This style was viewed as meaningful only within the psychosocial context, that is, in the interaction between the child and his or her caretakers. This perspective does not a priori guarantee behavioral consistency over time, or even setting, since the qualities of interaction might be changing all the while.

Criticism based on theoretical and empirical grounds has been directed toward a behavioral style approach to temperament (Bates, 1980; Lamb, 1980; Persson-Blenow & McNeil, 1979). It is clear to many that the procedures employed in the early phase of the NYLS, and the peculiar nature of the sample itself, seriously limit its generalizability and replicability. Indeed, since the mid-1970s, with the appearance of

TABLE 3.1

Definitions of Thomas and Chess's Nine Temperament Dimensions

Activity level: the child's typical motoric activity within an array of daily activities, including eating, dressing, play, and bathing.

Intensity of reaction: the overall level of energy in the child's response.

Rhythmicity: the regularity of sleep or waking patterns, bowel movements, and hunger.

Adaptability: the child's response to novel or changed situations or events, including the duration of the initial response.

Threshold of responsiveness: the level of stimulation necessary to evoke a response from the child.

Persistence and attention span: the length of time the child will continue to pursue an activity or persist despite obstacles.

Distractibility: the degree to which environmental stimuli can change or redirect the current activity of the child.

Quality of *Mood*: Pleasant, joyful behavior versus unpleasant, crying or complaint behavior.

Approach/Withdrawal: Positive versus negative responsivity to new stimuli, including objects, situations, and persons.

SOURCE: Thomas and Chess (1977, pp. 21-22).

competing theoretical and methodological approaches, the original nine categories Thomas and Chess constructed have been modified and interpreted in several important ways. Proponents of a behavioral style approach to temperament appear to be rather unsurprised by evidence of high mutability or lack of stability over time in temperamental differences. Such a pattern of results in other research domains would be quite unsettling (for example, intelligence data). Thomas and Chess describe their perspective on temperament as largely *phenomenological*, in that it is subject to contextual and developmental alterations and not clearly tied to a specific etiology. Of course, such a view of temperament fits well with what longitudinal data we have concerning the continuity of their nine categories. In summary, there appears to be only moderate to negligible correlations for these temperament dimensions across four or more years duration (Plomin, 1982). However, such a view may actually sidestep the more difficult questions concerning the integrity of the temperament concept across time. It may also be that the constitutionality-based definition of temperament through history is so qualitatively distinct from a behavioral style view that it is misleading to incorporate the two under the same rubric.

The notion that something about temperament must be stable for it to be a useful and operational construct is reinforced by Buss and Plomin's (1975) approach. *Stability* would be a critical factor in studies attempting to point out the heritability and predictive utility of individual differences. The highly interactional view of temperament espoused by Thomas and Chess suggests that stability can only be identified by better attention to the changes in context and development or, in other words, a more sensitive measurement model matched to the complexity of the phenomenon. Plomin has offered his view on this issue:

> It is a truism that both an organism and its environment are prerequisites for behavior. In order to understand individual differences, however, the important question is the relative extent to which societally important phenomena can be explained by characteristic styles of temperament, by differences in experiences, and by temperament-environment interactions. This is an empirical and as yet unanswered question. Although any measure of temperament includes the products of former temperament-environment interactions, to measure temperament as independently as possible of the environment is a reasonable goal. These measures become the operational definition of temperament, the starting point for research. (Plomin, 1982, p. 39)

Buss and Plomin's perspective originally lead them to hypothesize that at least four dimensions of temperament can be identified. These are (1) *Emotionality*, (2) *Activity*, (3) *Sociability*, and (4) *Impulsiveness* (EASI). Subsequently, however, these researchers chose to eliminate the Impulsivity dimension, claiming that it failed to meet the specific criteria concerning heritability and continuity. Other works that draw upon this view have primarily utilized genetic studies to investigate the heritability of such dimensions with mixed results (Goldsmith & Gottesman, 1981). However, there is a consensus among many in the field that data from parent questionnaires such as the EASI suggest moderate heritability does exist for several dimensions. Measures of temperament characteristics arising from Buss and Plomin's theoretical approach have emphasized the observation of child behavior, which manifests each of these four basic dimensions. These researchers developed a parent questionnaire that attempts to tap the four dimensions (EASI; Buss & Plomin, 1975) and another questionnaire that incorporates their dimensions with some of the NYLS characteristics (Colorado Childhood Temperament Inventory; Plomin & Rowe, 1977).

In more recent years Plomin has employed structured observations within laboratory settings in an attempt to garner independent evidence for the existence and stability of his original dimensions. He has argued that more carefully controlled observation within defined contextual situations might reveal important data concerning individual differences. The research on temperament in the late seventies and early eighties has reflected this trend away from sole reliance upon parental reports across a broad range of situations. Some of these research studies have based observations on Nancy Bayley's *Infant Behavior Record* (Matheny, 1980; Matheny & Wilson, 1981), in some cases using videotaped behavioral data elicited within structured situations or tasks designed to tap hypothesized temperament dimensions.

Temperament characteristics studied by Wilson and Matheny (1983) include attention span, activity, emotional tone, cooperation, and orientation to staff. These researchers have begun to demonstrate that convergence between lab and home-based temperamental characteristics can be shown. Their early results suggest that a continuity across contexts may exist for a "biobehavioral lability," which is reflected by "fluctuations in emotional tone and activity and on nonrhythmicity of vegetative functions" (p. 181). The ultimate aim of this line of inquiry is to differentiate those characteristics that appear to be less affected by factors such as developmental maturation or contextual influence from other temperament characteristics that can be substantially altered or transformed as the child grows or the environment changes. Since these investigators study twins there is a suggestion that presumed heritable characteristics may be demonstrated as well.

Another perspective on temperament is exemplified in the work by Rothbart and Derryberry (1981). Their theoretical approach appears to be exceedingly comprehensive in that few imaginable factors are left out of their model to explain the nature and course of individual differences. At the core of their theory are two elements. First, they postulate that there are important linkages between biologic substrata, such as the *reactivity* of the autonomic nervous system, and higher-level mechanisms of affect, motivation, and cognition. They argue that the interdependencies of psychological and biological systems provide the basis for temperament. Second, they point out the importance of a theoretical view that recognizes the interplay among affective, motivational, and cognitive domains in the expression of temperament and they question the degree to which such factors can be logically or operationally separated. The inclusion of cognitive factors and their influence on temperament goes against the grain of previous work in this area, most of which viewed the two as distinct and *pure* constructs. However, Rothbart and Derryberry argue that a separation of these two concepts is impractical and simplistic.

> It should be clear that in order to understand temperament conceived as individual differences in reactivity and self-regulation, we must also understand the infant's rate of maturation and level of cognitive development, and we have much to learn in this area. (Rothbart & Derryberry, 1981, p. 394)

The notion of a biological basis for temperament echoes back to the work of Pavlov (1955), Strelau (1969), and Berlyne (1960). While this approach may be appealing because of its emphasis on physiology and its comprehensiveness, few data are available pertaining to its validity, especially as it relates to infants and children. A key criticism (Goldsmith & Campos, 1982) has been that such a broad model may not allow the construct of temperament to become operationalized in empirical research. The main value of this perspective currently may be heuristic in its ability to designate psychophysiological parameters useful in laboratory-based measures of child behavior. It is generally agreed by most researchers that these measures will be crucial if we are to garner scientific credibility for the concept of temperament.

RELATED RESEARCH APPROACHES

All of the work summarized above has been included under the rubric of temperament research. Other research is pertinent to the construct of temperament inasmuch as it investigates processes that may be intimately associated with individual differences. However, these approaches are often not included in summaries or reviews of temperament research. We would like to briefly discuss a few approaches that will eventually emerge as important to the study of temperament.

Individual Differences in Neonates

Brazelton's development of the Neonatal Behavioral Assessment Scale (1973) has lead to numerous studies of temperament-related behaviors in infants and within interactions between caregivers and babies. While the scale and approach this group has offered was not intended as a temperament measure per se, many of the constructs used are similar to other notions we have discussed previously. These include aspects of the infant's social competencies, self-control in the face of distress, activity level, and rhythmicity. However, the Brazelton approach emphasizes the physiological aspects of infant behavior that are manifest within response characteristics in interactions with others (for example, mother and father). The scale itself has drawn criticism from several quarters due to findings related to low stability of dimensions across multiple assessments, conceivably due in part to state changes in the infant, contextual variables, and inadequacies of the instrument (Sameroff, 1978; Goldsmith & Campos, 1982).

Subsequent research by colleagues of Brazelton has lead to some interesting insights into the factors that mediate the expression of temperament-related behaviors in infants. Tronick's (1987) work on face-to-face interactions between mothers and infants offers an interesting method for exploring temperament concepts within a laboratory-based approach. His more recent studies on the transfer of affect during infant-caregiver interaction is worth special mention given our interest in the etiology of psychopathology and the role of temperamental variables. Tronick, Ricks, and Cohn (1982) provide a discussion of their view concerning affective displays by the infant as effectively coordinating the social exchange with mother.

> The displays convey an emotional evaluation of the partner's action, the state of the interaction, and also signal the infant's direction of action. For example, smiles typically indicate a positive emotional evaluation and signal that the infant will continue his or her direction of action, whereas grimaces and frowns express a negative emotive state and a change in the infant's direction of action. (p. 83)

Within the perspective Tronick and colleagues provide, many of the behaviors conceived in temperamental terms are serving specific functions within the mother-infant interaction. This view is of course compatible with more general notions from Thomas and Chess concerning temperament as "goodness of fit." However, Tronick's research suggests that behavior in early infancy can predict competence at one year of age. Also, this work has emphasized the importance of maternal variables such as personality characteristics and maternal self-esteem in the development of interactional styles *and* temperament-related behaviors in the children.

Emotion and Early Temperament

Emde, Gaensbauer, and Harmon (1976) have investigated the affective development of infants and young children. They seek to relate behavioral and biophysiologic tracts of development within a *Genetic Field Theory*. This theoretical orientation can be traced to Spitz (1965) and has earlier origins in both Wernerian developmental psychology (Werner & Kaplan, 1963) and the broader *Gestalten* tradition. Their approach is a systemic view of human development that attempts to incorporate the organismic factors in growth and environmental influence to produce, once again, a more comprehensive and transactional viewpoint. Specifically, these investigators seek to empirically characterize the evolution of affect during early child development, describe the considerable range of individual differences, and eventually use this information to inform therapeutic and intervention programs for children and families. One particular class of behavior they have chosen for study is *fearfulness*, a construct not far removed from the *approach-withdrawal* characteristic found in temperament research, and akin to behavior measured in the *strange situations* paradigm in developmental psychology (Ainsworth & Wittig, 1969).

It is important to note that these authors have remarked more than once that they view the development of affect as primarily a *discontinuous* process. And they point out that this assumption is in concert with Freudian and Eriksonian ideas about human development. They use this notion to explain marked changes in affective expression that have been observed during the first five to seven years of life. It is valuable to know that these empirical attempts to describe the *normal* processes of affective development also serve to point out a rather wide range in individual differences.

We do not begin to do justice to this work here. However, the relevance of the empirical investigation of affect and its behavioral expression to a theory of temperament should be quite clear. Gordon Allport (1937), Buss and Plomin (1975), and others (see Goldsmith & Campos, 1981) have viewed emotional development as central to their conceptions of temperament and personality. Again, it very well may be that the more structured and objective measures that Emde, Goldsmith,

Campos, and their colleagues are developing will prove to be critical to an eventual understanding of early individual differences.

Social Competencies in Very Young Children

Another group of studies represents an interesting approach to temperament-related behaviors and have much to say about the complexity of both measurement and theory in this area. Drawing upon constructs quite similar to those found in temperament research, various investigators have attempted to describe the social competencies of very young children. For example, Clarke-Stewart and colleagues have reported a series of studies that seek to relate *sociability* behaviors in late infancy through the preschool period to changes in context and developmental level (Clarke-Stewart, 1973; Clarke-Stewart Umeh, Snow, & Pederson, 1980; Clarke-Stewart, VanderStoep, & Killian, 1979). Here again we find concepts and methods that parallel the temperament approaches we have already discussed. We also find comparisons with other studies of infants, as in Tronick's research on face-to-face interactions.

> Patterns of correlations between sociability to mother and to stranger and measures of the social environment were also parallel. Sociability to both mother and stranger was related to frequent positive interaction with a "good" mother who was sensitive, responsive, stimulating, and accepting; who used questions rather than commands; and who talked about other people and about the child in her conversations with the child—a language style that might have sensitized the child to interpersonal interaction. (Clarke-Stewart et al., 1980, p. 299)

Numerous other studies exist in the developmental literature that are relevant to temperament theories, including those focused on gender differences in children (Block, 1976), activity level in play behavior (Halverson & Waldrop, 1976; Buss, Block & Block, 1980), early social conflict (Hay & Ross, 1982), cognitive style (Kagan, 1966; Kogan, 1976; Lee, Vaughn, & Kopp, 1983), and self-regulation (Kopp, 1982; Block & Block, 1980). This area is, of course, too large to review adequately here. However, it of interest to note that each represents an approach that can serve to inform our conceptualizations regarding the nature of temperament in young children. It is of interest to note that many of these studies do not refer to temperament as a central construct. Rather, many researchers have found the concept to be overly global and have sought to operationalize specific aspects of individual differences within their designs and methods.

The Emerging Sense of Self

Another area of research relevant to temperament is now receiving increased attention after many years of neglect. The development of a *sense of self* has been the focus of work of several different investigators. George Mead's (1934) pioneering conceptualizations about self-perception have gained momentum in clinical practice recently through the innovative research of Selman (1980), Kegan (1983), and others. Jerome Kagan (1982) draws from several separate disciplines to produce a useful essay on this topic in which he concludes that universal aspects of the self are detectable as early as the second year of life. He also states that the development of self-awareness cannot progress within an environment devoid of objects and persons. This point alone is not particularly controversial. However, he goes on to argue that it may be merely the *presence* of these others and the fact that some form of feedback is provided to the child that is critical to the acquisition of a sense of self, and not necessarily the type or quality of that interaction.

> Perhaps no special class of social interaction is necessary for these competencies to develop. Perhaps all that is required for the capacities called "self-awareness" to appear is any information resulting from the child's actions and feelings. The neurons of the visual cortex require patterned stimulation in order to mature and permit the psychological competence of discrimination. But almost any form of patterned stimulation will do. (Kagan, 1982, p. 377)

As the reader might suppose, the notion that the self emerges from an interaction between the child and his or her environment (specifically the people and objects of that environment) resonates with notions in the main theoretical views on temperament we have discussed. The role of a developing sense of self, if indeed it is operant as early as the second year of life or earlier, implies that this sense could be highly influential in the behavioral manifestation of any temperament dimensions observable in the infant or young child. Therefore, it is likely that gradual and/or abrupt qualitative changes in temperamental display could be linked to an incremental sophistication of the child's internal mechanisms, as well as to other changes in developmental context or social environment. The discontinuities observable in many children across the first five years of life may not be due simply to a "goodness of fit," to use Thomas and Chess's term, and they may not be due to an ephemeral nature of early personality dimensions. Rather, the whole process appears to be one continually made more complex by the appearance and influence of cognitive, affective, and motivational processes in the developing child. For many children these mechanisms, and their amalgams, may critically mediate early temperament to produce considerable fluctuations in behavioral manifestation.

In light of this possibility, one must wonder if a theory of temperament that seeks to propose characteristics that are relatively pure, constitutionally based (in that they will be heritable and moderately stable), and empirically measurable may be destined to be sorely inadequate. One review of the issues involved in individual differences research, mindful of these significant problems, has suggested we limit our studies of temperament per se to the infancy period only (Goldsmith & Campos, 1981).

FROM THEORY TO METHODS AND MEASUREMENT

Parental Reports

Several useful reviews of various measures of temperament, reliability and validity data, and findings related to each, are available in the professional literature (Goldsmith & Campos, 1981; Hubert et al., 1982; Plomin, 1982). A point of particular interest in these various reviews involves the range of conclusions. Hubert et al. (1982) comment that "no single psychometrically sound and adequately validated measure of temperament is currently available" (p. 578). This is in contrast to Plomin's (1982) observation that "measures of temperament...generally show modest concurrent validity correlations of about .20 to .40" (p. 54).

In a recent application of three temperament questionnaires in a British sample of children aged 1-5 years, Gibbs, Reeves, and Cunningham (1987) report psychometric shortcomings in the Toddler and Preschooler versions of the Thomas and Chess approach as well as less than desirable characteristics in Plomin and Buss's EASI-1 questionnaire. And so it would appear that assessments of the psychometric status of temperament depend very much upon one's particular perspective.

Some observers have considerably more faith in the status of temperament methodology than others. This is not unlike situations found in other scientific disciplines and perhaps we can take solace in that fact. However, fewer examples can be found in which research has proceeded with such fervor prior to a careful, operational definition of the phenomenon of interest. Thomas and Chess's work, despite its method-ological weaknesses, was an attempt to describe the construct of temperament through a largely qualitative treatment of a particular domain of data, in this case, parental reports and impressions about their children. It is ironic that some fault their efforts with the suggestion that parental reports are actually distorted perceptions of reality (Bates, 1980) and apt to mislead us about the *true* nature of children. This argument challenges the essential theory underlying the Thomas and Chess approach, and has created yet another controversy among investigators in this area (Thomas, Chess, & Korn, 1982). However, this criticism goes hand in hand with a desire by many in the field for more objective and validated measures apart from parental sources (that is, lab-based observation in structured and unstructured situations; physio-logic indices). The approach to measuring temperament used in the NYLS reflects clearly a key theoretical assumption about the construct. For example, many items contained in the Parent Questionnaire for children 3-7 years of age (Thomas, Chess, & Korn, 1963) emphasize behavior within its psychosocial context, such as:

> *When in the park, at a party or visiting, my child will go up to strange children and join in their play.*

or:

> *When shopping together and mother does not buy candy, toys or clothing that the child wants, he/she cries and yells.*

Following Thomas et al.'s lead, Carey and McDevitt (Carey, 1972; Carey & McDevitt, 1978, McDevitt & Carey, 1981) have constructed measures based upon the original nine dimensions reported in the NYLS. Their work attempts to achieve a balance between the need for clinical relevance (Carey is a practicing pediatrician) and closer adherence to psychometric standards (McDevitt is a psychologist). Their questionnaires, typically administered to the primary caretaker, also tend to emphasize the child's behavior in social situations. Examples of items from their measures include the following:

> *The infant is shy (turns away or clings to mother) on meeting another child for the first time;*

and:

> *The child ignores parent's first call while watching favorite TV program.*

Some items on these measures do attend specifically to the quality of certain classes of child behavior when attempting to assess dimensions such as:

The child runs to where he/she wants to go (Activity dimension);

or:

The infant's bowel movements come at different times from day to day (Rhythmicity dimension).

Although the orientations of Thomas et al. and Carey parallel one another closely, the advantages of the parent questionnaires offered by the latter researchers are derived from their demonstrated psychometric characteristics. McDevitt and Carey (1981) report on item and scale construction, their internal consistency, test-retest reliability, and preliminary evidence for the construct validity of the various dimensions and their combinations. Because of this basic work, many now view their measures as the most appropriate for eliciting parent information using a questionnaire format. One issue has been raised, however, concerning the nine dimensions originally identified by Thomas and colleagues. Some research suggests these can be reduced in number to four or five dimensions that fit the data equally well (Plomin & Rowe, 1977; Scholom, Zucker, & Stollak, 1979), and that qualitative differences in the identity of dimensions found can occur as a function of social class and cultural context (Garrison, Earls, & Kindlon, 1984).

The reader should also be aware of other questionnaires seeking to measure separate dimensions of temperament. One has been offered by Rothbart (1981) that is based on six hypothesized characteristics: *fear, distress to limitations, laughter and smiling, soothability, activity,* and *duration of orienting.* Eventually, Rothbart hopes to assess the convergence of these characteristics with lab-based observations of temperament as in the Wilson and Matheny study. Rothbart's Infant Behavior Questionnaire consists of items designed to tap the dimensions listed above. Some examples of these items are presented below:

(1) "During feeding how often did the baby:
    lie or sit quietly?
    squirm or kick?
    wave arms?
    fuss or cry when s/he had enough to eat?
    fuss or cry when given a disliked food?"

(2) "How often during the last week did the baby:
     cry or show distress at a loud sound?
     cry or show distress at a change in parents' appearance?"

Plomin and colleagues have also offered a questionnaire approach to the measurement of temperament that is keyed to the *E*motionality, *A*ctivity, and *S*ociability dimensions. The Colorado Childhood Temperament Inventory (Plomin & Rowe, 1977) is a 30-item instrument for children aged 1-6 years. Consistent with a desire to capture behaviors relatively stable across contexts, the items on this inventory tend to diminish the specificity of temperament within interactions as in the Thomas and Chess questionnaire approach.

Other questionnaires exist that measure temperament dimensions or constellations but space considerations prevent us from going into detail regarding all of these. Perhaps the availability of numerous temperament surveys or questionnaires speaks to the variety of approaches that have characterized this field of study.

Measures Based on Behavioral Observation

Investigators of temperament are currently placing a great deal of emphasis on developing new measures that do not place heavy reliance upon parental reports. Many of these measures involve the observation of infants and children in structured or unstructured situations using rating scales keyed to various hypothesized temperament dimensions. Some of these methods arose from attempts to cross-validate parental reports, while other studies sought to maximize objectivity.

Use of the Infant Behavior Record (IBR; Bayley, 1969) has been reported by Matheny, Wilson, and colleagues (Matheny, 1980; Matheny, Dolan, & Wilson, 1976; Wilson & Matheny, 1983). While the IBR was originally intended as a behavioral supplement to mental testing with the Bayley Scales of Infant Development, Matheny and Wilson (1981) have adapted it to produce rating scales used in their structured *play vignettes* with infants and toddlers. Their work, the Louisville Twin Study, seeks to follow a sample of infant twins within a prospective longitudinal design to measure temperament more objectively and comprehensively over time. The specific vignettes employed in this study have been fully described (Matheny & Wilson, 1981). An example of standard play vignettes is presented below:

PUPPET

Behind *E*'s back. *E* puts on a hand puppet, and, after gaining the infant's attention, reveals the puppet. *E* describes the puppet, then initiates interaction between the infant and puppet: *E* may have the puppet "talk" and ask for a kiss and so on, or *E* may try to get the infant engaged in a conversation with the puppet. If the infant is willing, *E* encourages the infant to work the puppet.

MECHANICAL TOY

A battery-powered dog that barks and moves is placed in front of the infant. The controlling mechanism, connected to the dog by a long wire, is held by *E* who activates the dog, and, at the same time, shows the infant how the toy works. The infant is offered the control and encouraged to make the dog bark and move. If the infant does not take the control, it is placed on the floor within reach of the infant. *E* encourages the infant to get the control, but if the infant does not make an attempt within about 10 seconds, *E* regains the control and repeats the procedure.

HIDDEN OBJECT

The infant is seated at a low table on which two screens are arranged side by side. *E* introduces and demonstrates a small mechanical toy, offers it to the infant, and helps the infant to make the toy work. *E* then takes the toy and places it under one of the screens and asks the infant to find it. The procedure is repeated for the other screen. If the infant has not been successful on either trial, the sequence is repeated. If the infant is successful, *E* places the toy under the first screen, removes it and places it under the second screen. (Matheny & Wilson, 1981, p. 18)

Drawing upon the IBR, Matheny (1981) has reported on twin concordance for several dimensions emerging from factor analysis, including task orientation, affect-extraversion, activity, auditory-visual awareness, and motor coordination. Matheny, Wilson, and colleagues are now employing these dimensions within longitudinal studies of twins, a body of work that promises to provide much information about the nature of temperament and its sources.

Goldsmith (1982), Rothbart (1981), Plomin (1984), and Bates (1980) have also employed laboratory-based observations of temperament and descriptions of their methods are available in their reports. In each case, the studies have based laboratory ratings or observations on the theoretical perspective of the particular investigator. An important first step has already been taken as more investigators attempt to operationalize their conceptions of temperament and measure them directly. Since there are close similarities among the characteristics being studied, comparisons across studies emerging from this initial phase will be most useful. It is quite possible we may be able to reach a consensus as to the basic dimensions of temperament in infancy. Only then will there be a firm foundation for subsequent studies of change and continuity in temperament during the later years of child development.

Measuring Temperament
Across the Life Cycle

In a recent development related to the original NYLS dimensions, the work of Lerner, Palermo, Spiro, & Nesselroade (1982) has suggested that five factors may be most appropriate in self-description of temperament during each of three periods in human development (early childhood, middle to late childhood, and early adulthood). These are *activity level, attention span/distractibility, adaptability/approach-withdrawal, rhythmicity*, and *reactivity*. Their measure, called the Dimensions of Temperament Survey (DOTS), benefits from sophisticated psychometric construction with demonstrated internal consistency and test-retest reliability. Lerner et al.'s methods represent an exciting opportunity to go beyond the work of Thomas and colleagues. Their contextual model of temperament does not necessarily imply individual continuity, whereas Lerner et al.'s model would. Even though Thomas's and Lerner's group each stress a psychosocially relevant behavioral style, Lerner et al.'s approach argues for developmental stability with origins both in the person and in the similarities of various person-situation interactions.

> The *goodness-of-fit* model indicates that the meaning of temperament lies not in the child's possession of particular attributes, per se, but rather in the extent to which the attributes coincide with contextual demands regarding behavioral style. Because such demands may show age as well as setting variation, we chose ... to identify a set of temperamental attributes that do not show age variation across the age range of interest. (Lerner et al., 1982, p. 150)

SUMMARY

This chapter highlights some of the work and ideas that have typified research on childhood temperament during the past 25 years. As we stated early on, it is a field characterized by controversy and, to some degree, a lack of cohesion. However, important new directions have been initiated in recent years that suggest our entire approach to the topic of temperament will undergo significant alteration and improvement.

Demonstrations of *continuity* have been the goal of much of the work on temperament. This has included both *homotypic continuity*, which is stability over time for a particular construction of temperament (for example, the nine NYLS dimensions), and *heterotypic continuity*, as in the case of a hypothesized relationship between an early temperament dimension and subsequent behavior patterns. While most researchers have claimed low to moderate correlations across the first five to six years of life, there are few data crossing into middle childhood and adolescence. An educated guess would be, however, that such correlations using current methods would diminish as the child grows and that any clinical case prediction based on early temperament alone would be decidedly inefficient.

Other methodological issues in temperament research will continue to challenge us in the coming years and two of these are interrelated. First, we will need to formulate a consensus that parental reports of child temperament are very probably a mixture of *both* accurate information and parental biases. This mixture will not always be equivalent across studies, of course, in that some samples of parents may introduce more distortion than others due to their own characteristics (depressed mothers versus nondepressed mothers). But the suggestion that all parent reports are grossly off the mark seems quite unrealistic.

Related to this is the recurring question regarding the degree to which we are measuring characteristics of the child versus broad qualities of parent-child interaction. That is, when we ask parents to rate their child along dimensions largely representative of interactions specific to the context provided by parenting it is possible that we will have, in the end, data with limited generalizability across situations and time. If it is parent-child interaction we are truly interested in, then perhaps we should spend more time studying the families themselves and expend less energy trying to attribute the phenomena we measure to constitutionally based characteristics in the child.

Recent attempts to develop laboratory-based measures of specified behavioral constructs such as emotionality, activity, attention span, inhibition, and others may provide a more useful foundation for studies examining consistency across contexts. However, some of the data we have now suggest that even measures such as these will find sizable inconsistency in the child under 18 months of age, with rather dramatic shifts occurring during the first year of life. Of course, this trend may be reversed by better measures, or methods devised to aggregate behavior across situations, but we should be prepared to accept discontinuity when we encounter it.

This last point involving discontinuity is a crucial one for temperament methods and theory. At present, the only formal explanation for observed change in temperament across the child's early years is provided by the goodness-of-fit model. This would suggest that modification in temperament is probably a result of changes in the child's *match* to his or her environment (that is, parents). This model, as we have pointed out, tends to sidestep more difficult questions about the origins of temperament by attributing its course to rather nebulous aspects of a complex interaction. Within our theoretical musings about temperament there is a need to address *change* as a process unto itself. Attention to this aspect will be vital to the utility of more recent approaches to measurement.

Finally, we would be remiss if we did not emphasize an earlier point about the influence of an emerging *sense of self* in the child upon preexisting characteristics of behavior or *personality*. It may be that as the child grows, an executive function is developing that allows the child to perceive, organize, and interpret information about her own temperament (or the way in which she is behaving). This sense of self may, as time proceeds, exert more and more influence over the manifestation of temperament and contribute greatly to either the consistency or inconsistency we find. Of course, it is equally interesting to hypothesize that early temperament (once we can reliably measure it) may influence the development of the sense of self in very young children with implications carrying over into later years.

What can we conclude from all of this? Perhaps only that we have far to go. It is somewhat reassuring, however, that we seem to be letting go of our more simplistic notions about temperament and moving toward greater sensitivity to myriad complicated issues that must be addressed.

4

RELATIONSHIP BETWEEN TEMPERAMENT AND PSYCHOPATHOLOGY

Many researchers and clinicians who are interested in the concept of early individual differences or temperament typically hope to identify connections between measurable characteristics and concurrent or subsequent psychopathological conditions. Such associations will not be simply made and it is probably naive to envision a relationship between temperament characteristics and psychopathology in *direct* terms. This whole issue, however, is a central concern of many practitioners who work with children in mental health and pediatric settings. If answers to the complex questions surrounding this topic can be found, then they would serve to inform clinical procedures as well as social programs and policies that seek to aid young children and their families. The data concerning these issues are far from definitive, but they represent a stimulating collection of findings.

In this chapter we present the patterns of results reported by several key studies in this area. Also, we attempt to acquaint the reader with the multiplicity of factors that are probably involved in any relationship between early temperamental dimensions and concurrent or subsequent maladjustment. Most of the data pertinent to this question come from relatively short-term studies where measures were administered concurrently or over a span of from four to seven years time. Longer-term data have not been available, with the exception of the New York Longitudinal Survey, which recently reported a follow-up into the early adult years for 133 subjects. Since much of the scientific work pertaining to temperament has been based upon or inspired by the NYLS, it is perhaps fitting that we both begin and end this chapter with findings from that pioneering study.

THE CONCEPT OF THE DIFFICULT CHILD

Thomas and his colleagues identified several clinically useful temperament constellations in their original sample of infants. Most notably the
temperamentally *difficult child* has been a notion with much appeal to
researchers and clinicians working with infants and preschool-aged
children. As the reader will recall from Chapter 3, this pattern is com-
prised of high levels of activity, high intensity, low rhythmicity, and a
predominant negative mood. Other researchers have developed definitions of a difficultness constellation that generally conform to the
overall pattern of behaviors reported by Thomas and Chess.

Bates, Freeland, and Lounsbury (1979) describe their version of the
fussy-difficult infant as corresponding to the negative *mood* and high
intensity dimensions in the Thomas and Chess constellation. In older
children, Webster-Stratton and Eyberg (1982) describe the difficult
child in the terminology provided by Buss and Plomin's (1975) EAS
approach. Using the Colorado Childhood Temperament Inventory
(Plomin & Rowe, 1977), these investigators identified a constellation
defined by high *activity* and low *attention span/persistence*. Similarly,
Earls (1981) reports on a temperament constellation derived from factor
analysis of items on the NYLS Parent Questionnaire composed of low
distractibility, high *intensity* and low *adaptability*. He initially named
this category *distractibility-oppositionalism* but later Barron and Earls
(1984) renamed it *inflexibility*. These studies and their findings illustrate
methodological and theoretical problems in separating temperament
from behavior problems, an issue we will address later in this chapter.

Coining the term *difficult* to describe these children is in keeping with
an interactional perspective that implies the child is perceived as difficult
by someone else (that is, the parent). Typically this constellation arises
from the reports of parents or caretakers, and not from measures such as
time-limited behavioral observation in the home or laboratory setting.
This has lead some to view the construct of difficult temperament as
more representative of parental perception than a quality of so-called
difficultness in the child himself or herself (Bates, 1980).

Thomas and Chess (1982) and others have argued that viewing
temperament as merely perceptual data from parents is also simplistic.
They suggest that the parent can serve as an accurate observer of
children's behavioral attributes and are the best source for a quick
summary of child behavior across a broader range of situations and
time. They admit that parental distortion can and does occur in some

cases, but is not sufficient to warrant a general abandonment of the method. This controversy over the reality of the difficult temperament will remain until convergent validity between questionnaire-derived dimensions and other sources of assessment can be more fully explored. Unfortunately, the latter group of measures have not been fully developed as of yet though several are currently being tested (see Chapter 3).

It is important to include here that the Thomas and Chess position clearly states that some stability in their temperamental constellations can be shown, but they do not consider the nine dimensions and/or their combinations to be necessarily fixed or immutable. They point to both environmental and maturational variables that can influence tempera- ment and its manifestation across development. Therefore, those children who could not be categorized during the first or second year of life using a temperament typology might be successfully classified during later years. Also, children categorized early on as easy or difficult might move across the typology or become nonclassifiable because of changes in the environment (for example, improved "fit" between child and parent) or as a function of maturation (for instance, a biologically linked decrease in activity level).

Carey and McDevitt (1978) report findings from a study of 187 infants followed 3-7 years later with temperament questionnaires administered during infancy and at follow-up. The overall pattern of results suggests low to moderate continuity with roughly a quarter of the difficult infants categorized similarly at follow-up and a little more than a third of the easy children remaining within that particular constel- lation. Also, some cases demonstrate dramatic shifts from one temper- ament constellation to another while others show sizable changes in their relative values across each of the nine dimensions. This pattern of results has been generally replicated in a study of several birth cohorts of infants within a demarcated community in New England (Garrison et al., 1984). However, recent studies combine to suggest that the prevalence and reality of the difficult-easy distinction continues to be in doubt (Gibbs et al., 1987).

Controversy regarding the utility and reality of the difficultness concept has generally revolved around the view of parental reports as social perceptions and not as accurate descriptions of child behavior. However, other problems with the concept have been described. First, descriptions of difficult infants, toddlers, preschoolers, and older children have largely emphasized the behaviors manifest within adverse interactions. Difficultness has not been conceived in terms of cognitive dimensions such as frustration tolerance, generalized anxiety or other emotional states, or in situationally specific contexts that may modify the expression of temperament. Second, physiologic correlates of this concept need to be better formulated and examined with carefully collected behavioral observation and parent report data. Kagan's approach to the behaviorally inhibited child is a good example of this technique (Garcia-Coll et al., 1984). Others report correlations with identifiable biochemical factors in children such as in the association connection between dopamine-beta-hydroxylase (DBH) and the negative emotionality factor (mood) on the Carey questionnaire (Rappoport, Pandoni, Renfield, Lake, & Ziegler, 1977). Problems with continuity over time, however, continue to limit the longer-term value of the difficultness concept and seriously bring into question its importance.

TEMPERAMENT AND CHILD BEHAVIOR PROBLEMS

Concurrent Relationships

Despite particular biases regarding what difficult temperament is or how it should be measured, research is available on temperament's purported relationship to behavior disorders in young children. In some studies researchers have attempted to adhere to the original Thomas and Chess procedures for categorizing children's temperament. In other studies, sample-specific constellations are presented and analyzed in connection with behavioral indices.

Earls and his associates have reported on a concurrent relationship between temperament and behavior problems in children aged 3-7 years. Working within a normal population of preschool children, Earls (1981) found that low distractibility, high intensity, and low adaptability were three temperament characteristics associated with the presence of a moderate-to-high number of behavioral difficulties in three-year olds. He reports a particularly strong relationship between these dimensions and the total number of behavior symptoms reported. Barron and Earls (1984) further examined the concurrent association of temperament and behavior problems in the same population using additional variables as potential mediators of observed correlation. They report that temperamental *inflexibility* (a label for the constellation above) and poor parent-child interaction could each act to enhance a positive association between family stress (as measured through the presence of acute or chronic life conditions) and behavioral outcomes in the preschooler. Since items comprising the inflexibility dimension were, in terms of content, often indicative of the quality of parent-child interaction it could be argued each of these predictor variables were measuring slightly different aspects of the same phenomenon.

In a study by Webster-Stratton and Eyberg (1982), the concurrent association between temperament and behavior problems in 3- to 4-year olds was examined. They report that child temperament was related to both the presence of behavior problems and the quality of mother-child interactions. *Highly active* children with *low attention span* were especially noted to exhibit behavior problems to both parents and external observers. This study, despite a rather small sample size, did employ laboratory-based behavioral observations so as to measure interaction directly. This aspect of their study lends credence to their finding of a relationship between temperament as measured by a parental questionnaire and external indices of behavioral dysfunction. However, the purported temperament dimensions useful in character-izing the behavior of the children seen as problematic are very similar to an identified syndrome in child psychiatry and psychology, namely *Attention-Deficit Disorder with Hyperactivity* (DSM-III, 1980).

Thomas and Chess's (1977) work also suggests moderate positive correlations between certain temperament dimensions and indices of behavioral disorder. Low rhythmicity, high intensity, and low adapt-ability were especially indicated in both quantitative and qualitative assessments of data from their sample. This observed connection may be partially a function of collecting both kinds of information (tempera-ment characteristics and behavioral problems) from the same source, in this case the mothers of the children. This procedure may enhance the apparent association between temperament and behavior problems, but it could also diminish the association, as in the case of the parent who perceives the difficult temperament in a positive light. Alexander Thomas tells the story of the father who described his temperamentally difficult son as "lusty," a child others might view as problematic and bothersome.

In summary, each of the studies above suffer from considerable methodological problems, some of which are borne in a definitional confusion that spills over into methodology. First and foremost among these, there is considerable room for *confounding* among measures of temperament and behavior problems due to content similarity, as well as to the fact that measures have been typically administered at the same time and to the same source (that is, mothers). The Webster-Stratton and Eyberg study employed external observations of the children but these were not intended specifically to identify behavioral disorders. Still, their findings serve to illustrate some overlap between certain temperament constellations and recognizable behavior syndromes.

In a similar vein, data from a few studies indicate that parent-generated ratings of temperament may be less connected with the child's free play or peer-play behavior (Plomin, 1976; Plomin and Rowe, 1977) than they are to observed parent-child interactions (Dunn and Kendrick, 1980). This suggests that temperament ratings from parent question-naires may have special pertinence to child behavior as it specifically relates to parents. This pattern of findings, however, does not manage to solve potential confounding among measures of temperament and behavior disorder in young children. Earls (1981), aware of this problem, argues that attempts must be made to separate the two concepts:

> This study has attempted to disentangle temperament and behavior problems methodically at an age when they may still be inextricably intertwined. However, the distinction between temperament and behavioral problems is an important one relevant to understanding the etiology and persistence of behavioral disorders and their response to environmental manipulations, including psychotherapy. Only through longitudinal studies can the dynamic relationship between temperament, behavioral adjustment, and environmental demands be understood. (p. 373)

Longitudinal Studies

Longitudinal studies of the temperament-behavior relationship reveal several interesting findings. Terestman (1980) analyzed data from a subsample of NYLS infants with a special focus on the role of *mood* quality and the *intensity* of behavioral response in predicting adjustment during the nursery school years. She sought to relate these characteristics specifically to subsequent emotional distress and the need for psychiatric treatment in the children five years later. This study can be criticized for an unrealistically high proportion of clinical cases (47% of the children were labeled disordered), which probably inflated estimates of temperament's actual predictive utility. Cameron (1977) also analyzed data from the NYLS and reports that a combination of child temperament with parental management style resulted in improved prediction of subsequent behavior problems during early childhood. Here again we see a practical view of temperament that emphasizes both sides of an interpersonal exchange.

Graham, Rutter, and George (1973) studied a group of 60 children 3-7 years of age and followed them for one year after initially measuring temperamental differences and behavioral difficulties. They report that low *regularity,* low *malleability* (which overlaps with NYLS dimension *adaptability*) and low *fastidiousness* (not measured in the NYLS) were useful in predicting behavioral dysfunction in the children one year later. It can be argued that one year is too short a time to allow for change to occur within such a limited age span, but the design and methodological precautions used in this study boost its credibility.

Garrison, Earls, and Kindlon (1984) reported a follow-up study of 63 American children who were assessed temperamentally and behaviorally at three years of age and again soon after school entry (6-7 years). Their analyses indicate that clear differences in findings can emerge as a function of the particular source of report at follow-up. Specifically, maternal descriptions of temperament were found to be more strongly related to outcome measures as defined by mothers again at follow-up (that is, reports of behavioral problems) than to measures from teachers or external observers. Using a multiple-criteria outcome measure drawing upon parent reports, teacher evaluations and a blind, independent clinical assessment, the authors report that high *Intensity* and high *Persistence* helped to predict later maladjustment in these children. These dimensions were interpreted as descriptive of stubborn or oppositional children, perhaps a form of 'difficultness' with special relevance to the 3-year-old sampling frame. A more detailed study over the first three years of life has revealed the predominant role that temperament plays in the origins of behavior disorders. The predisposing role of certain temperament traits in relation to family adversity is much clearer in males than in females, however (Earls et al., 1987).

These studies suggest temperamental characteristics, or early behavioral style, can be related to subsequent behavioral dysfunction but the specific dimensions that appear to be important vary as a function of methods, sample composition, and the sources or contexts of evaluation at follow-up.

Temperament, School Adjustment, and Learning Problems

It is important to point out initially that no research suggests a sizable relationship between temperament and intelligence levels. To our knowledge, only a handful of studies are available that examine a possible relationship between temperament and cognitive skills (Wachs & Gruen, 1982; Plomin, 1985; Maziade, Cote, Boutin, Bernier, & Thivierge, 1987). These studies have generally indicated that some temperamental dimensions may be more closely related to cognitive factors than others, but that more general indices of intellectual functioning are only minimally associated at best. The Maziade et al. study is an exception to this general pattern of findings in that temperament constellation at 4 and 8 months of age (easy versus difficult versus intermediate) was found to be associated with I.Q. outcomes at 4 years of age. It is quite likely, of course, that intellectual functioning and capacity goes on to mediate the expression of temperament in subsequent social and contextual interactions. And we do know that intelligence level, for example, is important in psychological coping in children (Garmezy, 1980). However, we must reiterate that few studies have attempted to look at this most important question and our knowledge base is very small.

Keogh (1982) has reviewed several studies on the relationship between temperament and successful adaptation in school. She concludes that teachers' awareness of stylistic differences in child behavior often affect their interaction with such children. Thus temperamental characteristics are seen as important variables in determining the manner with which the teacher instructs and assesses many children. This notion implies that temperamental differences in children are detected very early in the school years by teachers and this subjective information may play a part in both the course of schooling and in teacher-child interaction. Although similar in approach to Thomas and Chess's model of goodness of fit, Keogh's suggestion is useful in that it shifts the emphasis away from extreme temperaments and the relationship to psychopathologic conditions and puts more emphasis on the ways individual differences can more subtly influence the child's broader environment.

Research by Martin and his colleagues (Martin, 1985; Martin, Nagle, & Paget, 1985) has also suggested that temperamental factors in the early school years can influence the ways in which teachers evaluate child behavior, develop attitudes about instructional strategies, and assess academic performance. Martin has pointed out that future studies within educational contexts will be most valuable if they draw upon longitudinal research designs and use several independent sources of evaluation. Similarly, he has warned that the use of temperament data in understanding the dynamics of child behavior in school settings and in planning educational interventions be tempered by a sensitivity to the complexity of the processes involved.

> As school psychologists consider utilizing the temperament concept in their work, a caution seems necessary. Explanations to parents and educators of the etiology of a child's behavior which emphasize simple minded univariate or main effect causations are simply inappropriate. Explanations which emphasize highly stable traits are similarly inappropriate. Temperamental variables are not highly stable across different environments; they are not always present at birth or during the first year of life; and they are probably not the dominant causative variable in the affective-social realm. Temperament undoubtedly affects behavior in very complex ways. In order to understand this complexity, applied psychologists must be conversant with the concepts of genetic causation as predisposition, the importance of goodness-of-fit between style and environment as a factor in development of behavior problems, and behavioral chains in which the child's reactions serve as both stimulus and response to caretakers. Such notions help provide a more realistic picture of the complexity of human behavior. (Martin, 1983)

Martin's caveat, of course, also applies to a wide range of practitioners in pediatrics, psychology, and child development, many of whom attempt to incorporate notions about temperament into their interventions with families and children.

Sobesky and colleagues have also reported on the importance of temperament characteristics in the teacher-student "fit" over more than one academic year (Sobesky, List, Holden, & Braucht, 1981; List, Sobesky, & Braucht, 1982; Sobesky, Braucht, & List, 1984). Using a comparison of teacher's exemplars of "best-fit" children (their definitions of "Easy" temperament children in the class setting), these researchers sought to estimate fit between the children and their teachers via a geometric distance computed mathematically. Students whose degree of fitness was good (that is, closer to the teachers' ideal) were rated as also having fewer behavior problems. Within the educational setting these researchers have proposed several distinct temperament dimensions. These include Plunging, Persistence, Reactivity, Awareness, and Activity Level. Using these dimensions, 14 types were identified in their samples. However, continuity across time was found to be rather low. For example, in a sample of preschoolers only 20% of the children were typed identically in two subsequent academic years. However, children remaining in the same academic setting (school placement) demonstrated somewhat higher stability but still below what might be preferred. Children whose temperaments were described as low on Persistence, Plunging, or both were typically viewed as poor-fit types. Most of the best-fit children were moderate to high on Plunging and Persistence. They also tended to be lower on the Reactivity dimension and were less easily frustrated by cognitive tasks. One additional finding of interest involves differences observed for males versus females. Boys were found to be more stable than girls in the good-fit category over one year, but girls showed greater continuity in the poor-fit category.

In a different vein, Scholom's work (Scholom & Schiff, 1980; Scholom et al., 1979) suggests a longer-term relationship between temperament characteristics in the first year of life and subsequent adjustment to school. Also, they report that learning-disabled boys as a group demonstrate temperamental differences when compared to matched controls. One serious problem with methods employed in both studies, however, involves exclusive reliance on retrospective reports of temperament. This procedure enhances the likelihood that distortion and bias will influence results. In a similar study, Carey, McDevitt, and Baker (1979) failed to find any differences between learning-disabled children and matched controls. Some earlier work had suggested a weak association between temperament and school adjustment (Carey, Fox, & McDevitt, 1977; Thomas & Chess, 1977). In both of these studies it is of interest that low Adaptability emerged as a significant correlate to impaired adjustment in a school setting.

Preschool Behavior Problems and
Subsequent Outcomes in School

As we noted in Chapter 3, there is reason to expect a certain degree of unavoidable overlap between measures of temperament and other indices of behavior. In light of this, a body of data that might be generally helpful to our current discussion concerns the relationship of early behavior problems in children to concurrent or subsequent adjustment in school. Coleman, Wolkind, and Ashley (1977) report no relationship concurrently and point to situational differences as a key factor in this finding (or lack of a finding). Also, Garrison et al. (1984) failed to find a longitudinal relationship between temperament or behavior problems at three years of age and *school achievement* levels in the first or second grade. They suggest that differences might be more likely to appear after the second grade, when educational demands and variations in achievement typically increase. This same study did relate low Rhythmicity, high Intensity, and high Persistence during the preschool years with teachers' negative behavior assessment of children in the initial grades.

Richman, Graham, and Stevenson (1982) report on a comprehensive longitudinal study of over 700 preschool children in a London borough. Although they did not measure temperament directly, they also indicate that overlap with behavior probably exists. They report that preschool behavior problems can be associated with maladjustment five years later, in just over 60% of the initially problematic children. They argue that this finding refutes the view of behavioral disturbances as transient in nature. These researchers provide several interesting links between specific preschool patterns of behavior and subsequent disorder, as in the case of a *fearful* three-year old who later appears as *neurotic-like*, or in the case of the *restless* preschooler who displays *antisocial* behavior in the early school years. They also suggest more powerful associations over time between early behavior problems and subsequent cognitive and linguistic achievements. Finally, this study also points to important differences in behavioral continuity as a function of gender, with boys' problems more likely to persist over time. Finally, Richman et al. suggest that *disturbed* family relationships appear to contribute mightily to the persistence of behavior dysfunction in young children.

In a smaller but similar epidemiological survey of children in the United States, Garrison and Earls (1984) suggest that while case prediction using only preschool behavioral data is probably ill-fated, interesting symptom-syndromal relationships can be charted during the preschool through school period for some children. That study showed that where continuity in behavior problems can be found to exist (in 56% of the disordered subsample at three years of age), certain early behavioral symptoms have greater predictive significance than others. For example, *management difficulties* and *sleeping problems* during the preschool period were respectively associated at follow-up with *externalizing* and *internalizing* syndromes as measured by the Child Behavior Profile (Achenbach & Edelbrock, 1978). Even though continuity across all subjects was found to be moderate, the presence of children's behavior problems, when continuous, did not demonstrate gross transformation in the particular form of symptom manifestation. This pattern of results is remarkably parallel to those found by Richman et al. (1982), although the American study failed to note any gender differences. Garrison and Earls (1984) also report a longitudinal relationship between mother's level of depression-related symptomatology during the child's preschool years and aspects of the child's self-evaluative outcomes three to four years later, a finding that merits additional study.

In regard to the overall utility of temperament or behavior measures in predicting subsequent adjustment, Chamberlin's (1981) review of the literature prior to 1980 concludes:

> Preschool characteristics by themselves are not very good predictors of future functioning in school and it is unlikely that more refined tests of the future will be much better. The data presented indicate that a child's functioning at any one point in time is a complex mix of interacting biological and environmental variables, which are difficult if not impossible to predict over any great length of time. (p. 124)

This pessimistic viewpoint was based upon research that often failed to define preschool characteristics fully, relied heavily upon mothers as the sole source for information, and typically had no theoretical basis for posing basic questions about continuity and change. Each of these three global limitations still characterizes the study of early temperament and behavior, but there is some cause to think that the picture will brighten. Increased utilization of laboratory-based measures of more carefully operationalized constructs of individual differences (such as those described in Chapter 3) will be seen in the coming years. Also, there is a consensus among leaders in this field that a more sophisticated developmental theory of early personality or behavioral style must be formulated that allows for both stability and transition in the longitudinal course of individual differences. To look for temperamental continuity across the life span with little or no attention to the changing context of environment and development is now perceived as overly simplistic and not in keeping with much of the empirical data at hand.

EARLY TEMPERAMENT AND ADJUSTMENT IN ADOLESCENCE AND ADULTHOOD

There are several large studies of the relationship between childhood characteristics and psychopathological outcomes in later years (Mellsop, 1972; Robins, 1966). In regard to the putative role of individual temperament, however, one study merits special notice. Thomas and Chess (1984) have followed 133 persons from their original cohort of infants into adolescence and early adulthood (18-22 years) to examine the evolution of behavior disorders. They report that the most predominant diagnoses involve mild to moderate adjustment disorders that typically subside with time. A few children were found consistently to display problems across the time span studied but these problems seldom required extensive psychiatric intervention. Rather, Thomas and Chess recommend early parental guidance as one factor in reducing the continuity of disturbance over time. Follow-up of children in their study whose parents received such guidance revealed high recovery rates.

The essence of the theoretical and practical gains deriving from the NYLS is captured in recent comments by Thomas and Chess (1984):

> *Goodness of fit* does not imply an absence of stress and conflict. Quite the contrary. These are inevitable concomitants of the developmental process, in which new expectations and demands for change and progressively higher levels of functioning occur continuously as the child grows older. Demands, stresses, and conflicts, when in keeping with the child's developmental potentials, temperamental characteristics, and capacities for mastery, are constructive in their consequences. It is, rather, excessive stress resulting from poorness of fit between environmental expectations and demands and the capacities of the child at a particular level of development that leads to disturbed behavioral functioning. (p. 8)

Despite Thomas and Chess's emphasis upon temperament characteristics as a key component within a multiplicity of factors, their own data suggest that the greatest amount of variance in behavioral development (as it pertains to disorder) is accounted for by variables they did not study. These factors include genetic and environmental influences, normal developmental transitions, and the idiosyncrasies of cognitive, affective, and self-perceptual phenomena. They report that only 34% of the variance in adult outcomes can be explained through reference to their early childhood measures. It is important to emphasize that these measures included not only temperament but also indices of parental conflict and the clinical status of the children at three years of age. This finding would suggest that temperament alone, at least as they have measured it, contributes very little to the overall goodness-of-fit model and predicts poorly over the first two decades of life.

One can deduce from the substantial body of work Thomas and Chess have given us that the long-term clinical outlook for both difficult infants and behaviorally dysfunctional preschoolers is an optimistic one. Not only do most children identified as behaviorally or temperamentally problematic recover by early adulthood, but they also seem to be favorably disposed to short-term, parentally focused intervention. If we use the NYLS as a basis, more time-limited longitudinal studies of behavior dysfunction in young children (as in Richman et al., 1982, and Garrison and Earls, 1984) might be viewed as capturing a continuity not fated to persist beyond adolescence or even middle childhood. This is quite possible, of course, but we must not rush to judgment on this question. It is quite likely that we will note sizable differences due to sampling factors, particularities in the assessment of dysfunction, and a host of environmental factors that were uncontrolled or unmeasured in the NYLS. Still, the prognostic utility of temperament dimensions in children during the infancy through preschool period does not appear particularly strong if we use current research as our guide.

SUMMARY

The dearth of studies now available on a supposed relationship between early temperamental characteristics and subsequent child disorder precludes any definitive conclusions on this matter. Data we do have, however, suggest a rather weak association that deteriorates as development proceeds. With the exception of Thomas and Chess's work, there are few published studies currently available that follow children into the middle to adolescent years to examine temperament-pathology relationships. This situation is probably due to difficulties associated with accomplishing longitudinal studies as well as a general reluctance to depend upon current measures of temperament in young children. There are signs, however, that more studies will emerge as a current wave of enthusiasm for this topic crests within developmental psychology and child psychology.

The studies we report here, all framed within the first six or seven years of the child's life, have rendered somewhat variable results. We have noted a consistent trend toward finding a contemporaneous association between certain temperament dimensions/constellations and behavioral disorder. However, we have pointed out serious methodological problems with these studies. In general, it appears that parents who report a high degree of conflict in their interactions with children on temperament questionnaires also tend to report significant amounts of behavior problems for those same children. This might be considered a situation of double jeopardy for the child to the extent that temperament and behavior questionnaires are measuring the same phenomenon.

From a longitudinal view of three to four years, there is evidence that some preschoolers who display extreme temperamental characteristics such as negative Mood, high Intensity, low Adaptability, or high Persistence, may be more likely to be seen as disordered during the early school years. However, the data also indicate substantial room for change appears to exist and that temperament alone is insufficient for either screening or prediction from the preschool period to subsequent development.

Drawing upon the backdrop provided by several large studies of the continuity of problem behavior in young children, we see that the particular manifestation of behavior may be rather consistent for those children showing overall continuity in atypical patterns. That is, those children who were identified at 3 or 4 years of age as behaviorally disordered and again so identified at 6 to 8 years of age, did not tend to vary in the broad form of their disorder. Thus high-stability children reported to be management problems by parents in the preschool period also presented externalizing or antisocial behaviors after school entry. However, in this group of studies considerable discontinuity and change was noted as well (in some samples more than 50% of the *clinically defined* cases).

If the reader might suppose that more careful definition and measurement of temperament characteristics will probably lead to stronger association between that concept and child psychopathology then we offer one last study for your consideration. Garcia-Coll, Kagan, and Resnick (1983) have identified a sample of 117 children identified as high or low on the dimension of behavioral *inhibition*. This characteristic is similar to other dimensions such as *approach-withdrawal* and *fearfulness* found in temperament research. The authors chose to study only those children at the extreme pole of this dimension to chart cross-situational and chronologic continuity during early childhood with an eye toward eventually relating this early appearing characteristic to subsequent development. This dimension, and the work they report, should be of interest to clinicians who are familiar with young children reported by parents as inordinately shy or withdrawn. There is some evidence from social psychology that shy children become shy adults (Zimbardo, 1977). However, there appears to be little empirical evidence to support the hypothesis that high inhibition, low approach, or atypical fearfulness in the early years necessarily augurs psychopathology or abnormal social functioning in the adult years. Rather, these persons may evidence lifetime consistency along this dimension (although a sizable proportion of them do not) that seldom interferes significantly with normal functioning. Kagan estimates that over 90% of his sample are children well within the limits of behavioral and psychological health. He hypothesizes that this particular individual difference among children (and perhaps other dimensions) effect rather subtle influences in development areas such as the breadth of interpersonal relationships or perhaps vocational choice.

We might take this view even further and speculate that the large proportion of children we study from heterogeneous normal populations will not evidence strong or even moderate effects from early temperament in later life. In fact, the role of temperament or early behavioral patterns in subsequent development may be a mediational one. That is, early dimensions *by themselves* probably contribute a minimal amount to explanations of psychopathology during childhood or adulthood. Their real utility may reside in demonstrations of critical temperament interactions with a host of environmental factors, which are in turn moderated by gender, age, social class, and the larger cultural context. Thomas and Chess's (1984) study certainly suggests that this may be the destiny of the temperament construct in a more adequate theory of developmental psychopathology.

5

TEMPERAMENT IN CLINICAL PRACTICE

CLINICAL ASSESSMENT AND TREATMENT

Applications

The validity of the techniques and theories we have discussed thus for is limited by our lack of knowledge concerning the continuities and discontinuities of various temperament dimensions that have been described in the research literature. At the present time clinical use of such an approach, especially in the area of prediction or prognosis, needs to be constrained.

However, the level of precision required in clinical application is quite different from that expected for a scientific theory. Thus the ability of temperament measures to describe current parent-child interaction and inform the practitioner about the nature of the problem can be useful despite the psychometrician's concern for exacting validity, reliability, and long-term stability. Also, we must point out, existing nosologies in child psychopathology practice suffer from some of the same problems as temperament questionnaires and the dimensions they render.

The methods used in temperament research can boast a certain amount of face validity inasmuch as they provide behavioral descriptions of children at various ages. In addition, if one adopts a particular approach consistently, then application of temperament questionnaires over time can allow the practitioner to chart behavioral stability or change for individual patients. Indeed, this is the application that William Carey has recommended within the context of pediatric medicine in the outpatient practice setting (Carey et al., 1977).

Adoption of a temperament approach may have certain advantages in some clinical settings where an emphasis on disordered behavior is inappropriate. Therefore, it may be received better by patients and parents and the context of treatment greatly enhanced. For example, Cameron (1982) has reported on an application of the Thomas and Chess approach in an organized health setting in which temperament data were used by health providers to identify potential problem areas in a population of mothers and children defined at elevated risk for problems during early childhood. This program appears to offer considerable clinical utility for both screening and intervention with heterogeneous groups of mothers and their young children. However, limitation in discriminant and predictive validity serve to raise questions concerning its benefits versus risks when used alone.

An additional application involves using temperament data derived for children and comparing them with similar information about the child's caretakers (parents or teachers). *Temperament matching* can be achieved in this manner, providing the basis for follow-up interviews concerning problems in poor caretaker-child "fit." Lerner et al. (1982) have provided an extremely interesting and useful technique along these lines. The Dimensions of Temperament Survey (DOTS) have several comparable versions all keyed to the same temperamental dimensions. The clinician can obtain temperament data about the child (from both the child and the parents), the adult's self-report, and the the adult's *ethnotheory* concerning expected or ideal characteristics for a child. Access to these data sources allows one to detect interactional nuances within the larger framework that temperament notions provide.

Another application of temperament techniques lies in the area of individual psychotherapy with children and adults. Many clinicians use checklists and questionnaires of various types to gain information directly from the patient's themselves. That information often is discussed directly with the patient in the context of evaluation or therapy. In other situations the information is not discussed but is considered by the clinician within the diagnostic process. Data rendered by many of the temperament questionnaires we have described can be viewed as impressions of the self based upon perceived, repetitive patterns of behavior in the individual. Indeed, many of the personality inventories currently in use (for example, 16PF) employ this same approach. Unfortunately, there are fewer instruments of this kind for children. The Personality Inventory for Children (Wirt, Lachar, Klinedinst, & Seat, 1981) is an instrument completed by parents with strong emphasis on psychopathology. Other instruments, such as the Children's Personality Questionnaire, a self-report instrument, does not offer the theoretical and longitudinal sophistication that we believe will emerge from temperament research in the next decade. We would hope that temperament questionnaires will eventually capture unique aspects of behavior and personality in children that behavior problem inventories cannot.

Work with families and couples might also draw upon the temperament approach to examine poor and good "fit" in human relationships. Indeed, this approach is not new to many professionals who couch their work within a systems or multivariate perspective. We would argue that use of the temperament questionnaires for adults, children, and their siblings offers a wealth of information that can be relevant to family evaluation and treatment.

Relevant Issues in Behavioral Assessment

Measures of childhood psychopathology suffer from some rather serious problems, and the clinical applications of temperament approaches do not escape these. First, the cross-situationality of child behavior has been clearly recognized in the research literature (Achenbach, 1980; Rutter, 1980). Second, the impressionistic quality of data derived from parents and teachers is part and parcel of the subjective approach to data collection. Not only are reporters of child behavior and temperament susceptible to contextual variations but they also introduce their own particular biases into the observations provided via checklist and interviews. Still, we tend to agree with Achenbach (1980) and others who argue that often such reports represent the most detailed and relevant information we can hope to obtain for many children seen in health settings. Parent's exposure to variation in child behavior over time and context leads to information that represents aggregated data. In addition, parents may be more likely to have observed certain hallmark symptoms whose absence or presence can significantly alter the diagnostic picture. Further, other major techniques for evaluation of child behavior—direct observation and clinical assessment—suffer from their own shortcomings, including limitations in time and context, "distortion" from particular theoretical or methodological vantage points, and notoriously poor concordance across individual clinicians.

In the absence of definite psychiatric symptomatology, clinicians are often faced with children who do not fall neatly into any broad, let alone narrow, nosologic category. At that point a descriptive, empirical approach must be adopted—that is, an approach that attempts to allow multiple sources of data to converge so as to create a more complete view of the child's behavior. (The reader is urged to read volume 3 of this series, *Assessment and Taxonomy of Child and Adolescent Psychopathology,* by Thomas M. Achenbach, for an excellent treatment of these issues.)

One final point regarding assessment of child behavior and temperament is warranted. It is very likely that certain transition points in normal child development affect the manner in which behavior problems are manifest and then defined by caretakers. For example, as the child achieves locomotion his or her activity and intensity characteristics can take on new meaning to the parents. In clinical practice it is not uncommon to hear parents tell of problems beginning when the child was able to walk about and "get into things." Similarly, the anxious or low-approach child may not represent a concern to parents, at least not at the level of seeking professional help, until the transition to preschool or alternative caretaking takes place and becomes a more regular source of concern. This again is a common problem in many settings that deal with young children and their families.

In infancy, the particular context for caretaking responsibilities leads to problems with children being defined in terms of the chief tasks for the parent: feeding, sleep patterns, and diapering routines. Finally, oppositional or aggressive behavior may be tolerated by parents until the point when the child comes into regular contact with peers or is under the scrutiny of other adults. As we can see in each of these cases, the temperamental quality may reside in the child for a longer period of time than the espoused history we encounter in the clinical setting. This phenomenon helps to explain why various researchers have developed somewhat divergent definitions of the "difficult" child depending upon the chronologic age or developmental levels of the children under study.

THREE PATTERNS OF CHILD BEHAVIOR

Because child temperament appears to be somewhat elusive to our current measurement techniques, we must approach the data we collect on the individual child with substantial caution. Further, elaborations of these data in the form of scores or numerical indices on dimensions or within sophisticated typologies are equally suspect. We have seen that the longer-term value of the concept of the difficult infant is almost negligible in most studies, although more value may derive from specific dimensions of temperament than clusters of dimensions. Similarly, those studies that have charted moderate to serious behavioral disturbances in older children have also reported limited predictive value over time. Thus we are left with a phenomenon that is mutable in ways we do not understand, and yet it presents us with problems in the here and now that must be addressed.

We would like to consider three broad patterns of child behavior that have been identified or alluded to in the clinical and research literature. Within the context of a discussion for each pattern, we will entertain notions concerning temperament and the potential value this concept holds for clinical diagnosis and treatment strategies. In this manner it is our hope that the reader will begin to grasp both the complexity and limitations involved, as well as the enormous potential such an approach may have for the individual clinical case.

High Activity Level

Problems deriving from excessive motoric activity level, and to a lesser degree short attention span, are quite common in those settings in which professionals come into contact with young children. Epidemiologic studies of preschool and early school behavior problems suggest that a rather large proportion of mothers view their children's particular activity level as a concern (Achenbach, 1984). This proportion is much too large to label all such children as psychiatrically or neurologically disordered. Still, American psychiatry has been criticized as too liberal with the criteria for identifying Hyperactivity Syndrome, Attention-Deficit Disorder with Hyperactivity, Minimal Brain Dysfunction, and so on (Rutter, 1983). This is thought to be largely responsible for the higher prevalence rates of this form of disorder in the United States as compared to the United Kingdom, Japan, and other sites of clinical and epidemiologic inquiry. Aside from this controversy, it does appear that a good proportion of parents in the United States and elsewhere consider the activity level of their children as excessive and problematic. This proportion is known to decrease as the child ages (Achenbach, 1978), and the peak percentages appear to fall between four and eight years of age.

Many factors influence this phenomenon, of course. Two brief clinical vignettes are provided to help illustrate some of these factors and the possible role temperament concepts play in both evaluation and treatment.

J. W. is a seven-year-old boy who was brought to a community mental health center via a school referral for "attention-deficit disorder." Currently in the first grade, J. W. had completed kindergarten with no reported learning or behavioral problems although his year-end teacher's assessment described him as a "spirited, curious and active child." J. W.'s first grade teacher provided behavioral information that indicated his activity level and disruptiveness was beginning to "irritate" the teacher and other children in the classroom. He was not having significant learning problems, however, and was reported to score above grade level in all academic areas as measured by available standardized test scores. J. W. was reported to be "somewhat fidgety" and would occasionally interrupt the class with questions or comments or would answer the teacher's questions out of turn. The teacher did not report any aggressive or antisocial symptoms and described the child as usually in a happy mood, seeking out interactions with other children, and as somewhat distractible in the large group setting.

J. W.'s parents reported that he presented few problems at home although he has always seemed "more active" than his siblings. Parents first noticed this tendency when J. W. began to walk but they managed to resolve problems with this characteristic as they arose through behavioral techniques suggested by paternal grandmother who reported that father had been the same way early in his development. J. W. was not reported to be impulsive or highly distractible by the parents. He was able to sit for prolonged periods of time at home, read books, and play alone contentedly. The parents also reported they were unaware of any problems with other children in the neighborhood or siblings. J. W. was also described by his parents as a "warm and loving" child. This perspective of the parents obviously gave rise to surprise and concern when the teacher contacted them and suggested professional evaluation.

Physical examination and neurologic screening were found to be normal. Formal psychometric testing of the child revealed cognitive capacities to be in the high average range with no significant weak areas and no suggestion of neuropsychological impairment. Projective techniques and direct interview of the child revealed no evidence for emotional disturbance, although the evaluator did remark that the child manifested some awareness of his teacher's dissatisfaction with his behavior. J. W. reported that he enjoys going to school, finds it interesting and fun, and has several good friends. Family history was not contributory with the expection of paternal grandmother's second-hand report regarding father's activity level in his early school years. The current family situation was judged to be stable and no significant life events or chronic conditions were noted. In fact, J. W.'s school-related difficulties represented the central concern in the parent's lives at that time.

Before we discuss this case let us consider another child who is described at referral in a similar manner.

S. C. is an eight-year-old boy referred to a neuropsychological clinic by his pediatrician for evaluation to "rule out hyperactivity syndrome and neurological dysfunction." The parents of S. C. had reported problems of various kinds to the pediatrician since birth and different approaches to these problems had been attempted over the past five to six years with little success reported. The child was now repeating the second grade, having evidenced significant behavioral and learning problems since kindergarten. Previous teachers had described the child as highly active with short attention span, disruptive in class, hyperaggressive, having poor peer relations, moody, showing temper tantrums, impulsive, accident prone, and displaying an array of additional behavior symptoms.

S. C.'s parents, who were separated at the time of evaluation, describe the child as very active, unable to sit for more than a minute or two at a time, unable to play alone or with a group of children for prolonged periods of time. The parents reported that S. C. was able, on occasion, to sit still to watch one or two television shows for about 15 to 20 minutes. Mother reported that S. C.'s problems with activity and attention span/distractibility were evident to her "from the very beginning" although the situation worsened when he began to walk. Mother also goes on to designate numerous behavioral symptoms for the child including aggressivity, antisocial behavior, primary enuresis, and a high level of accident-proneness. Indeed, the mother went on to report that she had brought the child "many times" to seek medical help for S. C.'s scrapes, falls, and other accidents. These visits had eventually led to an investigation for parental neglect by the Deparment of Social Services, which was later unsubstantiated. This experience, mother reported, now made her leery of contact with health care professionals.

Physical examination was unremarkable except for noted developmental delays in knowledge and social interaction. Subsequent psychometric data revealed a child with delays in school-related skills of approximately two to three years and a strong suggestion of neuropsychological dysfunction. The neurologist's evaluation of the child revealed several "soft signs of impairment including problems in visual-motor function, awkward gait, poor fine and gross motor planning, and generally high levels of activity, distractibility and impulsiveness on examination." The child was again evaluated using psychological tests and found to exhibit cognitive capacities in the low average range with significant differences (scatter) across subtests of the instruments used. The overall pattern of results from psychological testing led to an interpretation of neurologically based impairment manifest primarily by significant "deficits in attention-span, short-term memory, visual-motor integration processing, and low tolerence for cognitive frustration." Extra-test behavior was noted by the examiner to be "exceedingly active" and characterized by "an aggressive, confrontational style."

These vignettes raise some important issues concerning temperament and psychopathology. First of all, the symptomatology each child presents varies in both degree and the number of functional areas that are significantly impaired. However, each of the parents in these cases, along with various teachers who come into contact with the children, used the terms *attention-deficit disorder* and / or *hyperactivity*. Despite the comparable quality of the children's behavior, the functional differences are apparent on comparison. We would suspect that few clinicians would have prescribed a high level of intervention for the first child, although the second child might certainly have profited from a variety of treatments (a trial of stimulant medication, behavior modification, or family counseling). From the viewpoint of etiology it would be valuable to know whether or not these two children exist along a continuum of high activity level or whether they represent qualitatively distinct types: the first boy a temperamental variant while the second boy manifests a serious neurophysiologic dysfunction. However, if we judge that each child's behavioral pattern is a product of "a continuum of reproductive casualty" (Pasaminick and Knobloch, 1966), or of comparable neurologic structures gone awry, then we are left with this question: What is the value of this interpretation to the first child? Of course, some critics of biologic explanations for hyperactivity phenomena would suggest there is limited clinical value to the second child as well.

In any event, a practical question arises: What is the treatment or counseling approach for the first child who does not fit well into a psychiatric disorder category and yet is presenting in the clinic setting with a problem in need of remediation? Experienced health professionals who work with young children will recognize the pattern of the first child as a very common one in pediatric and community mental health centers.

At this juncture we would refer back to Thomas and Chess's model of temperament that emphasizes the behavioral style of the child and the fit between child and environment, primarily vis-à-vis the caretakers and the tasks presented to the child. These concepts are useful in an initial approach to advising the parents of the first child described earlier. To report to the parents and teachers that the child is completely normal is to invalidate their impressions and offers them little hope for change. Still, we would be wrong to label the child with a psychopathologic condition when this is not warranted. Parent counseling concerning the notions they themselves present the long-term quality of the behavior and the expectations for the ideal child, might lead to an adjustment in perspective that would represent a therapeutic gain. Also, instruction in simple techniques of behavior modification in the home and at school would be a reasonable first step in attempting to manage the child's disruptive patterns, all without presuming a psychopathological condition.

In the case of the second child, who presents with an array of cognitive and perceptual data to support a more serious pattern, treatment will differ somewhat but some of the principles deriving from a temperament model of behavior are useful here as well. For example, Barkley (1985a, 1985b; Barkley, Karlsson, Polland, & Murphy, 1985) has offered a perspective on hyperactive children that clearly demonstrates the role caretaker-child interaction plays in exacerbating or minimizing clinical outcomes. He argues that closer examination of the parental response to the hyperactive pattern in the child, regardless of whether or not the etiology of the disorder is known, can be most helpful in the design and implementation of behavioral treatment. He goes on to argue (1985b) that these interactional patterns probably influence the development of aggressive tendencies in the moderate proportion of hyperactives who demonstrate such behavior. Barkley bolsters his arguments and data with the observation that many children who meet criteria for Hyperactivity Syndrome or Attention-Deficit Disorder do not have a uniform behavioral presentation across situations, thereby reinforcing the notion that even for these children environmental forces mediate expression of the neurophysiologic dysfunction that probably underlies the general pattern.

The notions of temperament-environment interactions are well within the grasp of many parents. Emphasis on this model of child behavior can be a fruitful approach with the many young children who present with high activity levels, or are perceived as such by their parents, without creating either stigma or self-fulfilling prophecies through clinical intervention. For those children who clearly meet criteria for Attention-Deficit Disorder with Hyperactivity there is also value in the behavioral style approach even though a neurologic etiology may be involved.

Finally, there is additional value in the distinctions that a temperament approach provides concerning other dimensions that can effectively mediate the impact and meaning of high activity level. For example, the child in the first vignette was reported by all who came into contact with him to be pleasant and prosocial, although lacking in self-control and in need of regular supervision. These general comments translated into temperament scores in the direction of positive *mood*, high *approach*, and low *persistence* using the Thomas and Chess dimensions. However, the second child scored in the opposite direction along each of these dimensions and, of course, observers would render significantly more behavioral problems in addition to those subsumed by the hyperactivity. In purely descriptive terms, the environment's approach to the child via his or her caretakers will vary as a function of differences in other temperament dimensions and their combinations as well.

Oppositionality and Aggression

Somewhat reluctantly we include the pattern of oppositionality in this discussion, cognizant of the difficult issues and skepticism it has raised. From the outset we must acknowledge that the concept of the *oppositional child* as a psychopathological entity is on weak empirical grounds. Michael Rutter (1980) has likened the DSM-III disorder so named as akin to "spitting in the wind." Also, the name of the disorder itself implies as much about the quality of interaction as it does about characteristics in the child. Still, there is a rationale of sorts. Prolonged interactional difficulties between children and parents should qualify as phenomena worthy of clinical and research attention. The issues of discipline and the quality of relationship between parent and child arise again and again in settings where children are evaluated. Thus the category of Oppositional Child / Adolescent does have a utility in that it describes a fairly common dysfunction in human relations. In addition, one could argue that it has as much validity as several other minor psychiatric disorder classes found in the DSM system. However, by directing the label to the child we may do disservice to both the scientific credibility of the taxonomy itself and to the purposes and intent of a scientifically based approach in child mental health.

And yet the pattern must be dealt with in clinical practice. Many practitioners would rightly place such dysfunction within the context of relations in the family. In some cases, however, clinicians might argue that children build up response patterns, or personality characteristics, that lead them to "test limits" and challenge parental or adult authority with a regularity that both impairs functioning and represents a quality of the child. For example, Olweus (1979) and others (Garrison, 1984; Monahan, 1984) have theorized that the behavior of certain highly aggressive adults and children is motivated by internalized response tendencies or neuropsychological factors that cannot be directly linked to aspects of the immediate environment. Similarly, it is an interesting notion that child behavior or personality can manifest antisocial tendencies early on in development. This has been suggested in the study by Richman et al. (1982) with preschool children. The etiologies of such a pattern are not clear but temperament concepts will probably constitute part of an eventual explanatory model.

In an excellent review on pathological unsocialized aggression in children, Frankel and Simmons (1985) discuss the variety of intrinsic factors that may account for this extreme pattern. Various characteristics such as *poor impulse control* (Messer, 1976), *hyperactivity* (O'Leary, 1980), and *persistence of behavior* (Patterson, 1975) appear to differentiate the expression of aggressive behavior. While a large amount of attention has been placed on the extrinsic contingencies surrounding aggressive behavior in children, clinical work with children has long operated on the hypothesis that the expression of aggressive impulses in some children is not solely controlled by identifiable environmental factors. At present, several perspectives on internal sources of aggression are being entertained including cognitive deficits in information processing, increased activity levels, atypical endocrine secretion and regulation, and perhaps neurologically or experientially caused deficiencies in verbal and empathic response. It will be of interest to include analyses of temperamental variables in longitudinal studies of children defined at risk for displaying physical aggression and patterns of oppositionality.

In a study of temperament characteristics and behavior problems in a cohort of three-year-old children Garrison, Earls, and Kindlon (1984) report data relevant to this discussion. As we explained earlier, the definition of difficultness in temperament seems to change somewhat as the child moves in and out of certain important transition points during early development. In the case of these three-year-old children the temperament constellation with the most predictive utility, in terms of forecasting those children found to exhibit a clinically defined pattern of behavioral disturbance at age seven, was a combination of two temperament dimensions. Using the Thomas and Chess system for describing temperament, Garrison and associates reported that those preschoolers high in *persistence* and *intensity* were much more likely to present with problematic behavioral symptoms across three different contexts at follow-up. As we noted in Chapter 4, an item analysis of these dimensions revealed a pattern that might be viewed rationally as one of *stubbornness, single-mindedness,* or even an *oppositionality* pattern especially when the child was in pursuit of a goal (such as obtaining a toy, demonstration of a preference for certain activities, and so on). We pointed out that the behavioral descriptions for these two dimensions were quite similar in tone and content to descriptions of behavior problems in children. Still, the temperament instrument used in this study attempted to measure repetitive patterns of behavior generalized across settings and contexts, although we have pointed out that the source of report does introduce a certain level of bias. Most behavior problem inventories, however, choose to focus on apparently discrete symptoms presumed to be related at the syndromal level.

We are left with several important and challenging questions. Is such a pattern a psychopathological disorder? Is it a temporary or contextually specific pattern? What is the influence of temperament characteristics in the development of such a pattern? Consider these questions as you review the following case:

F. A. is a nine-year-old girl residing in a middle-class suburb of a major city who was brought by parents to a clinical psychologist for persistent attitudinal and behavioral problems. She was at that time a fourth grade student who had achieved relatively high grades throughout her school career. Parents reported that the child had a wide cricle of friends, was active in several clubs or activities, and had never had any major physical health problems of any kind. The presenting problem, as the parents defined it, involved persistent negativism in the face of parental and teacher authority. F. A. was described as a rather stubborn and oppositional child and the parents traced the pattern to her toddlerhood years. They reported that the "terrible twos turned into the horrible threes." The parents had sought assistance from several sources including popular books by experts in the field of child psychology and pediatrics, consultations with their own pediatrician and a family counselor, and various relatives and friends who came into contact with F. A. None of these approaches or sources had led to much alteration in the child's oppositional stance to parental and teacher authority. After further probing, the parents revealed that the oppositional behavior typically resulted from their blocking a desired goal of the child's, but they reported this could be both "big things" (that is, material possessions or activities) and "little things" (choice of television programs, dinner selections, which clothes to wear).

Teachers' reports depicted a child who was performing at high levels academically, was popular with peers, demonstrated leadership skills in groups, and appeared content much of the time in school. However, teachers also reported that the child presented a moderate opposition to their requests in class, problems with conformity and compliance with rules, and some occasional temper outbursts followed by immature behavior, especially when refused a desired activity or object. It is important to note that the degree of difficulty varied somewhat across several teachers who provided reports; however, all agreed that F. A. presented an oppositional stance to adult authority in school settings. Parents and teachers would remark that F. A. would "see how far she could go" to circumvent demands of authority figures.

The child's home situation was judged to be stable with no gross marital of familial dysfunction evident. The results of formal psychometric testing performed by the psychologist was generally unremarkable although "testing of limits" was observed during the evaluation sessions.

In this case example we can detect several aspects that recur in clinical work with children with behavior problems. First, there is the parental impression that the child has always represented a difficult child although the severity and behavioral manifestations have not been clearly constant across the various phases of early childhood. Second, the child's behavior in this case has a pervasive quality across contexts in which an adult authority sets demands or expectations on the child's deportment. Third, an absence of overt psychopathology, family dysfunction, and significant life events in the child's history reduces the likelihood that these sources will be implicated in a presumed etiology. Finally, the overall level of impairment in the child's current day-to-day functioning could not be considered to be major. Still, parents decide this to be a problem significant enough to seek professional help. The pattern of behavior portrayed by the parents is repetitive and interfering with positive social interaction with other family members. The overall pattern also represents a risk factor for future problems of a more serious nature. At this juncture we must ask whether or not anything is to be gained by interpreting this pattern within a behavioral style frame of reference. Also, treatment strategies in such a case will vary as a function of the particular orientation of the clinical practitioner. However, the practical goal of a treatment plan should include initiating change in the child's repetitive response pattern to authority in her environment without necessarily presupposing that a psychopathological process underlies her behavior.

Suppose we view the child's behavior as a generalized style she has adopted in response to adult demands, the etiology of which we can only speculate about. This notion may have greater relevance both to the level of seriousness of the problem and to possible solutions or interventions than other hypotheses we might entertain concerning environmental influences. In addition, for those clinicians who place a good deal of emphasis on the child's individual ability to control or manage his or her own behavior, such a view would be useful.

Shyness and Social Withdrawal

A third behavioral pattern we would like to consider involves what has been variously referred to as the shy or withdrawn child. Kagan and his colleagues (Garcia-Coll et al., 1984) have referred to a similar phenomenon in young children as *behavioral inhibition.* It is a broad pattern that characterizes the behavior of a sizable proportion of the general population and is commonly presented as a behavioral problem in health settings for children. Some have argued that shyness is a phenomenon well within the normal range of behavioral functioning in children and should not be viewed as pathology. Others have pointed out that this pattern, like any gross pattern of child behavior, should be viewed as pathological when it represents a significant impairment to functioning. The exact relationship of this early behavioral manifestation with other psychiatric symptoms is unclear. Longitudinal studies of shy children do not indicate significantly greater proportions of diagnosable dysfunction. However, in the clinical setting, practitioners are more apt to see children who are experiencing impairment in one way or another (which is defined by parents as significant), and may display related symptoms such as depressed mood, schizoid social qualities, elevated anxiety levels, and others. Consider the following case example:

> L. B. is a nine-year-old boy seen in a school-psychologist's office with problems described as involving social interaction, isolation from peers, lack of interest in play activities in school, and a general pattern of withdrawn or shy behavior. Parents and teachers initiated the referral following a school conference.

> Parents reported that L. B. had evidenced a shyness and fearfulness of social situations from the preschool period. The initial months of day care when L. B. was three years of age were described as problematic in that the child cried each morning when left, and teachers would report he would remain aloof on the playground and in small-group interactions with other children. For advice the parents brought the child to the pediatrician, who felt the child would "grow out it," and encouraged the parents to continue the day-care experience. Kindergarten was characterized by a similar experience although the child cried and protested during the first two weeks. Following that he would willingly, although not enthusiastically, go off to school each morning. No appreciable absences were due to feigned illness or difficult behavior. Parents went on to describe the child's social circle as quite small, consisting of two friends who lived in the neighborhood with whom L. B. played infrequently. The child would not indicate a desire to play with these or other children with much frequency, although on occasion he would seek out these children.

> The parents went on to report that the child presented with few symptoms along the dimensions of aggression, depression, anxiety, and others captured by a behavioral inventory for children. They also reported that L. B. seemed to prefer being by himself and could play for hours in his room alone.

> The family was judged to be stable, although some significant life events were identified in the past. These primarily involved the parents or family as a whole; the parents could not identify events or chronic conditions affecting the child in particular. The physical examination of the child, developmental and neurological screening, and academic achievement of the child were found to be in the normal range. Psychoeducational evaluations by the school psychologist reveal a child who is guarded and quiet during testing. The psychologist goes on to report no significant cognitive or perceptual problems as measured by standardized tests. She then referred L. B. to a child psychiatrist for further emotional evaluation. The psychiatrist deferred diagnosis based upon an interview with parents and child, citing insufficient symptomatology to derive a definitive clinical syndrome.

Mother reported that the child had always been cautious or suspicious when put in new social situations or settings and when meeting new people. She described L. B. as "overly dependent" during the toddler and preschool years, protesting whenever the mother would leave him, even for a matter of hours.

Father reports that the child behaves much the way he did for much of his life, telling the interviewer that he "grew out of it in high school." However, in light of the teachers' concerns regarding L. B.'s social adaptation and apparent lack of interest in peers, both parents are seeking guidance about the nature of the pattern and possible interventions to improve the situation.

This child's withdrawal from peers and adults other than his parents clearly is creating problems with adaptation. Also, the child's sense of self appears to have been compromised by a lack of successful social experiences in the early school setting. Further, the parents indicate that the overall pattern of shyness and low approach in social situations is a long-standing problem both in the home (when strangers arrived) and outside the home. Still, using DSM-III or other nosological and empirical systems we would be hard-pressed to assign a particular psychopathological condition to this child. Again, as in the previous cases described, many clinicians would hazard a guess that this child is at risk for more serious problems if some level of intervention is not introduced. Some might leave this child to his own resources, given that the research literature suggests a good prognosis, or at least one that is not characterized by psychiatric disorder. In either view, however, it is clear that the child and the parents are experiencing significant concern over the causes and the consequences of the behavioral pattern. It would be inappropriate in this case to advise them that the child is well within the normal range and that problems will eventually subside.

Let us briefly consider some other contributions to the temperament research literature before discussing a possible intervention approach. First, Buss and Plomin (1984) have offered a useful distinction between shyness and sociability. *Shyness*, they point out, refers to behavior with people who are casual acquaintances or strangers. Such behavior might be characterized by increased anxiety, distress, and some avoidance of the situation or persons to decrease subjective discomfort. *Sociability*, on the other hand, refers to behaviors that are relevant to social affiliation with others as opposed to a preference for being alone. Because of this distinction and other evidence, Buss and Plomin have advised that shyness not be considered a temperamental characteristic, choosing instead to emphasize sociability. More recent studies by Plomin and colleagues (Daniels, Plomin, & Greenhalgh, 1984; Plomin & Daniels, 1984) suggest that persons who have a long history of shyness since infancy and a family history of such a pattern may represent a genetic subtype. Further, in the Colorado Adoption Project infant shyness was found to be related statistically to adult sociability at comparable levels as with shyness (given Buss and Plomin's distinction). Infant shyness in their sample, however, did not appear to be connected to adult emotionality or neuroticism. Deriving from work on the topic of shyness, Plomin and Daniels (1984) offer the following observation:

> Because we see no reason to uphold the stereotypic notion of the American as an extravert, we suggest that there is room for greater recognition of and respect for individual differences in shyness. Part of understanding our children and ourselves lies in recognizing genetic predispositions that distinguish us from other people. A nice feature of heredity in relation to childrearing is that like begets like—shy parents are likely to have shy children on the average, and shy parents also are likely to be accepting of their children's propensity towards shyness. We can accept these differences in ourselves and in our children rather than assume that deviations from the norm are necessarily aberrant. (pp. 16-17)

From a rather different research approach, Kagan and colleagues have proposed a descriptive classification of children who demonstrate a pattern of behavioral and physiologic inhibition in behavioral and physiological terms (see Chapter 3). The prototypical child described in their work appears to conform more with shyness than sociability and indeed only a relatively small percentage of the children in their study display moderate to severe psychiatric symptomatology or significant impairment in social functioning. A good proportion of the children classified as inhibited in the second year of life go on to resemble an uninhibited pattern a year later. The long-term outlook for such children, it is supposed, is quite good despite displaying rather distinct behavioral and physiologic differences from the norm earlier in development.

In the earlier case we see that the little boy is described as both shy and unsociable, having made few significant friends outside of the parents and siblings. Thus using Buss and Plomin's distinction, the child does not present a shyness pattern only. Consider also Michael Lewis's study of attachment behavior and subsequent behavioral dysfunction in young children (Lewis, Feiring, McGuffog, & Jaskir, 1984). In his study insecurely attached one-year-old boys were found longitudinally to display more "psychopathology" (that is, behavioral symptoms on the Child Behavior Checklist) than securely attached boys. Might we not refer to the parents' reports concerning early separation from mother as particularly difficult and consistently problematic in the first two years of life as a harbinger of continuing problems later on? Lewis et al. wisely point out that infants are probably not doomed to psychopathology via early manifestations of attachment quality, but that this variable, like many others, represents one ingredient in a multiplex of factors including situational, familial, and demographic variables.

The practitioner working with the child described earlier has few "leads" along these lines, and may be forced to focus on the style characteristics of the child and the resultant interactions with others as the initial emphasis for intervention. There is another interesting issue within this case that involves the possibility that the child is in a premorbid phase of a diagnosable dysfunction such as *Schizoid Disorder* or *Overanxious Disorder* (DSM-III). Time and appropriate longitudinal studies hold the ultimate answer to this question, of course, and if the clinician becomes overfocused on such speculation the efficacy of treatment will most definitely suffer. In light of the comments of numerous temperament researchers who are sensitive to the clinical issues of such children, the wisest course in such a case would be, again, to consider the interaction between the child and his or her environment and the effects of goodness or poorness of fit. In fact, it is within these interactions that target behaviors for change will exist. This can be done along strict behavioral lines, through temperament matching and counseling, through individual work with the child that promotes personal control of behavior, and other techniques that choose to emphasize the stylistic qualities of behavior and its consequences.

SUMMARY

In each of the clinical patterns that we describe above the role of temperament notions can be useful in both formulations about the nature of the problems and in treatment planning. We must recognize that the field of child psychopathology is one that, in developmental terms, approximates toddlerhood. We have yet to develop suitable taxonomies to capture the range of phenomena that are encountered in clinical settings. We would suggest that the generalizations concerning person-environment interactions and their role in the development of psychopathology will become more detailed as additional studies based on consensually agreed-upon nosologies are completed. We would argue that notions concerning early temperament, be these couched in physiological, genetic, interactional, or combinational terms, will emerge as important concepts in etiologic, diagnostic, and treatment models in child behavior dysfunction and psychopathology.

6

SUMMARY AND CRITIQUE

MAJOR RESEARCH AND CLINICAL ISSUES

Temperament Theory

Variation in definitions of temperament has led to considerable difficulty in comparing methods and findings from an array of studies purporting to explore the same phenomenon. Close inspection of several major approaches to the concept of temperament reveals that many investigators are, in essence, attempting to identify constitutionally based characteristics of persons that contribute to the overt expression of behavior. The operational definitions and dimensions these researchers have employed continue to vary, however, and this has diminished the cohesion we would like to see in the field. However, our review of the dominant approaches in this area suggests that a certain amount of overlap and replicability can be found. And, we would propose, the differences can often be rationally explained.

For example, certain differences in approach and findings appear to arise from the fact that some of the theoretical formulations that guide temperament research are influenced by the particular age or developmental levels of the children under study. The developmental tasks of each phase of childhood create a somewhat different collection of demands on the child and parent that in turn produce different foci for definitions of both temperament and behavioral problems. These alterations in developmental context include those of *infancy*, with intensified caretaking demands (such as feeding, sleep cycles, diapering, and so on); *toddlerhood* and increased locomotion; and the *preschool* period, with its common transitions to an expanded social world (via day care or organized educational settings). Depending upon which period of childhood or context for behavior various researchers and theorists have chosen to study their particular approach and the resulting data have been influenced.

Similarly, the original goals of each research approach have shaped the theoretical orientation. In the case of Thomas and Chess, attention was focused on behavior problems and early signs of psychiatric dysfunction and so temperament items and dimensions were fashioned in such a way that this aspect is a predominant theme. Also, their reliance on the reports of parents concerning child temperament and behavior as a primary source of information about the children probably helped to form their eventual perspective of temperament as a transactional product. Given the increasing emphasis in their work on children growing up within the context provided by parents, Thomas and Chess adopted a less organismic view of temperament and referred instead to a behavioral style. This notion of a style conforms with the longitudinal data they report and the apparent discontinuities in their hypothesized dimensions across both time and context.

Buss and Plomin's approach, on the other hand, reflects a desire to capture those characteristics that serve to define heritable and somewhat continuous influences in rather broadly defined human personality. Coming from a behavioral genetics and adult personality mode of thinking, these theoreticians are less occupied with finding links to disorder than they are with establishing the constitutionally based building blocks of human behavior patterns. Thus the dimensions they offer in their approach are necessarily globalized: sociability, emotionality, and activity level. They recognize fully that other concepts are subsumed by these categories of human temperament and that some will have more import for the study of disorder than others.

The psychobiologic perspective that Rothbart and colleagues represent again emphasizes organismic origins with a primary focus on infancy. This approach uses two broad concepts as its basis: physiological arousal and reactivity and its regulation by the self. Their model has also been criticized as broad and difficult to operationalize and measure, especially as the nature of temperament becomes more complex as development proceeds. However, one would be foolish to deny that temperament very probably does come under the direct and indirect influence of affective, motivational, and cognitive-developmental systems. Still, for such a theory to be of clinical value, it must be translated into methods that will ultimately help to predict aspects of behavior and dysfunction in individuals or groups.

Goldsmith and Campos's (1985) approach comes closest, along with Buss and Plomin's more recent articulation of their ideas (1984), to representing a confirmable theory of temperament in that their definition is an operational one and the assumptions testable to a greater degree than others we have discussed. Goldsmith and Campos also provide exclusional and inclusional criteria that force the researcher to devise measures that will, at least conceptually if not practically, tap relatively pure dimensions of temperament. Finally, their suspicion that the study of temperament per se may need to be limited to the infancy period provides an avenue that may render greater clarity in future research. However, if we adopt such a view we will need to formulate new models and theories for explaining temperament within children beyond the infancy period.

Robert McCall (Goldsmith et al., 1987) has attempted to provide temperament researchers with a synthesis of the various theoretical approaches to early temperament. He advises that a uniform definition of the concept is critical to future scientific research. Also, he emphasizes the need for identification of characteristics that have "relative consistency" over time and contexts, arguing that a purely interactional or environmental explanation moves considerably away from a consensus view that temperament should be thought of as a set of species-general "dispositions." A careful reading of the recent round-table discussion on temperament (Goldsmith et al., 1987) fully illustrates the essential difficulties in addressing all of the conceptual concerns of the various theories and approaches. Despite McCall's valiant effort to bring ideas together in a meaningful way it appears that, to some degree, various researchers are pursuing qualitatively different phenomena all being included under the rubric of temperament. We are somewhat more skeptical regarding how close the field may be to an agreed upon definition. Therefore, attempts toward synthesis will need to continue.

Special Relevance to Psychopathology

At this juncture we would like to reiterate some important points that derive from an overview of various theories of temperament that have special relevance to the study of child psychopathology. First of all, it is important to realize that most of the researchers in the area of temperament would not currently portray the concept as providing significant illumination to our understanding of the etiologic process of psychopathology. Rather, its current value resides in its emphasis on individual differences and within a potential to provide measures and ideas concerning the early characteristics of children. Descriptive and normative data concerning the very young child's expression of biologic characteristics in behavior will be invaluable to those who are interested in establishing baselines for children under study. However, we have not yet reached this point. Twenty-five years of research and theory have lead us to believe that discontinuity rather than continuity largely characterizes the personalities or behavioral response patterns of young children, at least with the methods we have used. However, in the study of disordered behavior in children, especially more serious forms, there appears to be relatively greater continuity, at least in the time frame provided by shorter-term studies we have reviewed here. However, even this observed continuity in behavioral disturbance holds limited prognostic value. As we have noted, theories of psychopathology also have far to go prior to achieving adequate explanatory and predictive validity. And they will remain significantly dependent upon the contributions of theories of normal development.

Theories of temperament are wrestling with several key problems found in the study of psychopathology. The major ones include the primacy of nature versus nurture, the relative importance of aspects of the emergent self (vis-à-vis cognition, perception, motivation) versus environmental forces in the control of behavior, and the transience or permanence of specific behavioral dimensions over time. In addition, it has been argued elsewhere (Wenar, 1982) that we do not have a truly developmental theory of psychopathology. We would suggest that a central component of such a theory will be derived from the study of temperament in the normal child.

At present, however, temperament notions do not fit well into developmental schemes or descriptions of behavior. Since the concept of development implies change, it would seem obvious that we should be spending a good amount of our efforts looking for discontinuities in behavior or temperament as well as continuities. The concept of temperament does not, in current models, have sufficient integrity concerning all aspects of child development to bind together the major approaches we have discussed in this book. Some redefinition will be required. We might consider defining temperament as constitutionally based characteristics that can be measured behaviorally only during some relatively brief time in infancy, or as those that can be linked to measurable physiologic phenomena. In addition, these characteristics might be expected to demonstrate heritability, although some will conceivably derive from the individual's prenatal and perinatal events or conditions.

As the child's environmental experience accrues, the term *temperament* may no longer be appropriate if we mean to imply qualities having distinct biological origins. At this point, theory might need to shift greater emphasis upon the manner in which earlier temperamental dimensions now manifest themselves within the current developmental and environmental context. Thus ideas about parent-child transactions and behavioral style become useful, and explanatory models that emphasize the interplay among various psychological domains appear more adequate. The idea of a behavioral style should not be viewed as very different from the concept of *generalized response tendencies* that researchers in other areas have employed. More sophisticated ways of looking at the characteristics of situations will also aid us in clarifying specific factors in environments that shape or mediate earlier temperamental qualities to derive a particular style across contexts.

When self-perception begins to become more apparent through development of cognitive, affective, and motivational systems in the child, the emerging sense of self may begin to serve an executive function that influences how temperament will be manifest in a manner just as powerful as the environment. And, at this point, such a developmental model brings us a considerable distance from notions about constitutional characteristics present at birth. And yet, it is a model such as the one we sketch here that will be necessary to account for both continuities and discontinuities in personality.

Of course, the importance of contextualism in early personality research is not a recent discovery (Bem & Allen, 1974). Also, recognition of the interplay that must occur among various domains, such as cognition and affect, has been long acknowledged in the determination of behavior. However, empirical research on temperament and child psychopathology has not generally addressed these questions. Rather, the emphasis has been upon finding stability in areas where our theoretical speculations and empirical data now suggest they may not be discernible.

Research Methodology

We have already pointed out that deficiencies in temperament theory directly affect the adequacy of our methodology. There are several areas where intensive effort will need to be expended if the concept of temperament is to have significant scientific relevance to the study of psychopathology. First, instruments purporting to measure temperament must seek to minimize the obvious and subtle overlap with measures of psychopathology. For example, more recent questionnaires have attempted to accomplish this by carefully wording items to capture more global behavior patterns rather than aspects of behavioral or interactional problems. In a related vein, it is important that such measures not seek only to measure the negative aspects of temperament. Positive mood as well as negative mood provides valuable information; the 'easy' child is of equal interest in understanding eventual normal and psychopathological outcomes within a comprehensive theory of temperament and psychopathology. Knowledge about a child's persistence in the face of adversity or frustration with a task is just as important as persistence in the context of parent-child conflict. These measures should attempt to establish concurrent validity through comparison with laboratory or clinical indices with known scientific or pragmatic significance.

Unlike others who have criticized the use of caretaker reports as the basis for measuring temperament, we recommend that our progress will be seriously limited if we do not use such data. The utility of temperament measures in large, prospective studies of heterogeneous samples of children will be greatly diminished if these measures are not time and cost-efficient. And, we would argue, it is within large representative samples of children that we will derive our most useful information concerning the development of psychopathology (in the largest proportion of the child population).

Hubert et al. (1982) suggest that we develop methods for transforming impressionistic data from parental reports into specific behavioral "cues and weights . . . to develop new scales" (p. 581) that would represent the ways in which parents define their children as easy versus difficult, for example, or as active versus inactive. Through a fine-tuning of instruments, drawing upon parental reports to render more sensitive behavioral data, a greater consistency in findings concerning the relationship between temperament and parent-child interaction may result. Also, we may enhance reliability coefficients for child temperament dimensions across diverse settings. Lerner's approach using the Dimensions of Temperament Survey also offers a useful distinction between the expectations of the ideal or normal child and the parents' impressions of their own child. The fit between the expected characteristics and parentally perceived qualities should reveal much about the process through which concepts such as the difficult child are derived. These methods are promising and may help to resolve the critical issues concerning the purportedly phenomenological nature of parent reports.

Behavioral genetics as a strategy for learning more about temperament and psychopathology is just beginning to realize its potential. Findings emerging from projects such as the Colorado Adoption Project (CAP; Plomin & DeFries, 1985) are exciting and stimulating to new research initiatives. The suggestion from the CAP data that environmental influences are mediated genetically provides a new perspective on relationships among variables that until relatively recently had been depicted in a more straightforward manner. The question of whether genes "drive" behavior or provide the background that eventually becomes obscured continues to motivate research using behavioral genetics methodologies. In line with our recommendations above, we would suggest that this approach to temperament might adopt methods that will allow for the study of change as well as stability in development. Such studies should look for heritability in the process of change, perhaps through indices sensitive to timing, rapidity, and magnitude in developmental alterations.

Laboratory-based measures of physiological and behavioral indices of temperament will provide a cornerstone for approaches eventually used in the field. Creative techniques are being devised to tap hypothesized temperamental dimensions and will lead to even more innovative notions about the phenomenon itself. One particular task within the development of laboratory-based measures is to derive a set of referent behaviors that might serve to anchor hypothesized temperament dimensions. Such behaviors might allow the researcher to recognize stability of temperament despite alterations in overt behavioral manifestation. For example, the toddler's behavioral display of approach versus withdrawal within a novel situation might entail gross motor behaviors in a much more dramatic manner than the adolescent's. The older child's manifestation of this temperamental dimension might be better analyzed within verbalizations and more subtle nonverbal behaviors such as posturing, gaze, and so on. Yet in each situation the researcher's referent behaviors involve social engagement versus avoidance. Finally, the linkage of physiological or biochemical measures to observed behavior will allow us to be more certain about the inferences we necessarily make regarding the meaning and functions of behavior.

Clinical Applications

An understanding of the diagnosis and treatment of psychopathology in children will eventually profit from the study of temperament and the insights it will offer. Within clinical groups of children several concepts deriving from temperament-related research will be particularly useful. We are especially hopeful about the current work that is examining the ontogeny of emotions in very young children typified in studies by Emde, Gaensbauer, Harmon, Goldsmith, Campos, and their colleagues. A merger between this approach to emotional development, notions that derive directly from temperament studies with normal children, and more traditional ideas concerning the etiology of pathology will serve to detail further the processes involved in developmental psychopathology.

Clinically, the concept of *emotional lability* has been entertained for many years in various forms and within an array of theoretical explanations. And so it is with great interest that we see such a concept arising from temperament research with at least some stability over time. There are some additional clinical hypotheses that may be useful in regard to the study of emotionality, especially as it relates to variation in responsiveness to environmental distress. The concepts of *fixation* and *regression* are invoked often within psychodynamic formulations that attempt to explain apparent discontinuities in behavior and development. This clinically derived view proposes that the child's current psychological functioning can appear age-appropriate, stagnated, or retrogressive as a function of external or internalized stress. These may also prove to be valuable constructs in future theoretical work concerning temperament and pathology. Along similar lines, influential theorists such as Gesell, Freud, Erikson, and Piaget point out that development can be largely characterized by periods of both stability and instability. This pattern was depicted as the natural course of normal developmental progression. Aside from alteration in child characteristics, which arises from variations in developmental maturation, it is likely that some discontinuity is caused by the interaction between environmental stress and the sense of self. Thus notions about fixation and regression in an ego-psychological framework may eventually complement more basic research and theory on temperament and psychopathology.

In a similar vein, the work on shyness, behavioral inhibition, and fearfulness clearly augments psychopathologists' attempts to understand the origins of disorders of social affiliation. The view that the child's temperament acts upon the environment to construct a *niche* that then maintains his or her characteristics is an interesting one. Further, a recent study of young inhibited children (Garcia-Coll et al., 1984) indicates that these children evidence higher heart rates as stress is introduced in the laboratory situation and that they are more likely to avoid stress on a behavioral level. Even though such studies are focused on essentially normal children, it is of interest to explore overlap between their ideas concerning heightened physiologic response in such children and the clinical concept of *anxiety*. Thomas and Chess (1984) have argued, based upon a 15-year follow-up of their original cohort, that anxiety appeared to be secondary to symptom formation arising from child characteristics, parent functioning, and other environmental influences. Still, the relationships among the clinical construct anxiety, temperamental fearfulness, and behavioral inhibition provide an intriguing area for future research.

The ongoing controversy regarding the existence and nature of the so-called difficult child in temperament research is reassuring to those clinicians who wrestle with this conflict within their practices. Despite the current controversy regarding the exact meaning of parental reports concerning this quality in child behavior, it is unwise for the practitioner to dismiss parent perceptions as impressionistic and grossly inaccurate. Attention to this temperamental constellation promises ultimately to benefit our understanding of the definition, natural course, and eventual significance of a scientifically elusive yet clinically relevant construct. At present, however, the difficultness quality of child temperament and behavior should be conservatively viewed as a salient, aggregate term that largely captures negative emotionality and adverse interactions between the parent and child. However, new methods may provide radically different definitions that portray difficultness as mediated by environment, physiology, genetics, and development. Indeed, studies such as those reported by Maziade et al.(1987), in which difficult temperament was associated with intellectual outcomes in young children over a four-year span, will require models that incorporate these various factors. Also, the suggestion that child temperament characteristics can influence family lifestyle and parents' personal decisions is a research line worthy of much greater attention (Galambos & Lerner, 1987).

We would especially like to see more studies exploring the relationships between the construct of difficultness in overt behavior and neurologic or psychoneurologic factors. Some interesting perspectives are emerging from a small number of researchers who have reported on a co-occurance of symptoms in clinical samples of neurologically impaired children and adults. For example, Denckla (1983) and Weintraub and Mesulam (1983) have noted certain sociobehavioral and emotional problems in children who also evidence significant neurologic signs of dysfunction in the cognitive, perceptual, and motoric domains. They suggest that these clusters of symptoms in their patients represent a distinct neurological syndrome. Because of a dearth of studies on the relationship between cognitive-perceptual factors and temperament, clinical and developmental psychology have little to offer in this area.

Similarly, work that has attempted to relate biochemical substances such as DBH (Rappoport et al., 1977) and plasma progesterone (Weissbluth, 1983) to child temperament represent an exciting direction for basic research. Finally, new methods for studying an array of biochemical, electrophysiological, and behavioral variables during sleep may augment our understanding of the significance of temperament, physiologic factors, and nocturnal cycles on daytime behavior in children (Weissbluth, 1981, 1982a, 1982b).

CONCLUDING REMARKS

Much of the work completed thus far on temperament and psychopathology constitutes the study of subclinical patterns of behavior. Whether or not these patterns have value in the prediction of psychiatric disorder or more serious forms of dysfunction remains to be seen. However, it will be important to shift our immediate focus from psychiatric illness and develop methods for classifying and observing patterns not currently viewed as psychopathological. These might include subclinical symptom patterns relevant to the development of intimacy, identity formation, subjective discontent, subclinical symptom patterns, and difficulties in social affiliation and adaptation. Such an approach may be particularly appropriate for children given developmental aspects of early psychopathology, and could bridge the gap between temperament dimensions or behavioral style, and more traditional ideas about psychiatric illness that have been largely formulated in the study of adults.

As stated previously, theory that attempts to relate temperament or early personality characteristics with subsequent psychopathological conditions will need to attend to several key factors. These include the child's ability to reference the self through cognitive-perceptual and affective apparatuses. We would propose that research on the developing sense of self in the young child will help to connect temperament data to a new perspective that informs us about the manner in which early characteristics and experience combine to influence adult personality and psychopathology.

Another important class of variables will be the genetic and biologic contributions of various familial (that is, caretaker's mental status and temperament characteristics) and early physiologic events (such as prenatal and perinatal trauma, illness, and so on) to the manifestation of temperament in the young child. Finally, researchers who seek to relate temperament with psychiatric disorders in children will need to take into account the dialectical relationships among environmental context, developmental timing, and biologic input. The Colorado Adoption Project directed by Plomin and DeFries, described in Chapter 4, is an excellent example of a study that attempts to address these major variable classes within a powerful research design.

Despite our emphasis on the more traditional medical model in understanding childhood psychiatric disorder and our suggestions regarding the potential value of more data on temperament and physiological and genetic factors, we would like to emphasize an additional and extremely important point. The field as a whole must recognize the inherent dangers if the nature-nurture pendulum swings too far back toward biologic factors. Just as the prior focus on the environment as the exclusive shaper of human personality now appears narrow, an unbalanced view placing biology at the fore will hardly be able to account for empirically derived facts that implicate the role of environment and person variables. For example, we must continue to recognize the powerful effects of poverty as a risk factor in the development of childhood behavior and developmental problems, as well as psychiatric illness.

In summary, conceptualizations regarding a connection between temperament and psychopathology must continue to strive for greater specificity at both ends. Fortunately, progress is being made in this regard by developmentalists and behavioral geneticists interested in temperament, and psychiatrists and psychologists interested in psycho-pathology. One fairly simple way in which the two may be associated is in the idea that some types of psychiatric disorders constitute deviations in personality development. For example, behavioral activity level represents the most straightforward case in which a normally distributed heritable trait may develop into maladaptive characteristics resulting in impaired learning and social relationships. When more extreme forms of psychopathology are thought of—those incorporating bizarre or dangerous aspects of behavior—the connections to temperament becomes more difficult to entertain. However, it is conceivable that even schizophrenia is heralded by certain temperamental traits that could be used as risk indicators or prognostic signs. So, continued efforts to establish connections between temperament and psychopathology may indeed be fruitful as the sciences of genetics, neurobiology, developmental psychology, and clinical psychiatry converge on understanding the basis for certain specific types of disorders of emotions, language, and thinking.

REFERENCES

Achenbach, T. (1978). The child behavior profile, I: Boys aged 6-11. *Journal of Consulting and Clinical Psychology, 46*, 478-488.

Achenbach, T. (1980). DSM-III in light of empirical research on the classification of child psychopathology. *Journal of American Academy of Child Psychiatry, 19*, 395-412.

Achenbach, T. (1984). *Developmental psychopathology*. New York: Ronald Press.

Achenbach, T., & Edelbrock, C. (1978). The classification of child psychopathology: A review and analysis of empirical efforts. *Psychological Bulletin, 85*, 1275-1301.

Ainsworth, M.D.S., & Wittig, B. (1969). Attachment and exploratory behavior of one-year-olds in a strange situation. In B. M. Foss (Ed.), *Determinants of infant behavior*. New York: John Wiley.

Allport, G. W. (1937). *Personality: A psychological interpretation*. New York: Holt.

Allport, G. W. (1961). *Pattern and growth in personality*. New York: Holt, Rinehart & Winston.

American Psychiatric Association. (1980). *Diagnostic and statistical manual of mental disorders* (3rd ed.). Washington, DC: Author.

Barkley, R. (1985a). The parent-child interaction patterns of hyperactive children: Precursors to aggressive behavior? *Advances in Developmental and Behavioral Pediatrics, 6*, 117-149.

Barkley, R. (1985b). The social behavior of hyperactive children: Developmental changes, drug effects, and situational variation. In R. McMahon and R. Peters (Eds.), *Childhood Disorders*. New York: Brunner/Mazel.

Barkley, R., Karlsson, J., Pollard, S., & Murphy, J. (1985). Developmental changes in the mother-child interactions of hyperactive boys: Effects of two dose levels of ritalin. *Journal of Child Psychology and Psychiatry, 26*, 705-715.

Barron, A., & Earls, F. (1984). The relationship of social and temperament factors in behavior problems in three-year-old children: A cross-national replication. *Journal of Child Psychology and Psychiatry, 25*, 23-33.

Bates, J. (1980). The concept of difficult temperament. *Merrill-Palmer Quarterly, 26*, 299-319.

Bates, J., Freeland, C., & Lounsbury, M. (1979). Measurement of infant difficultness. *Child Development, 50*, 794-803.

Bayley, N. (1969). *Manual for the Bayley Scales of Infant Development*. New York: Psychological Corporation.

Bem, D., & Allen, A. (1974). On predicting some of the people some of the time. *Psychological Review, 81*, 506-520.

Berlyne, D. (1960). *Conflict, arousal and curiosity*. New York: McGraw-Hill.

Block, J. H. (1976). Debatable conclusions about sex differences. *Contemporary Psychology, 21,* 517-522.

Block, J., & Block, J. (1980). The role of ego-control and ego-resiliency in the organization of behavior. In W. A. Collins (Ed.), *Minnesota symposia on child psychology* (Vol. 13). New York: Lawrence Earlbaum.

Brazelton, T. B. (1973). Neonatal behavioral assessment scale. *National Spastics Society Monograph.* Philadelphia: Lippincott.

Buss, D. (1984). Evolutionary biology and personality psychology: Towards a conception of human nature and individual differences. *American Psychologist, 39,* 1135-1147.

Buss, D., Block, J., & Block, J. (1980). Preschool activity level: Personality correlates and developmental implications. *Child Development, 51,* 401-408.

Buss, A. H., & Plomin, R. (1975). *A temperament theory of personality development.* New York: John Wiley.

Buss, A. H., & Plomin, R. (1984). *Early developing personality traits.* Hillsdale, NJ: Lawrence Erlbaum.

Cameron, J. (1977). Parental treatment, children's temperament, and the risk of childhood behavior problems. *American Journal of Orthopsychiatry, 47,* 568-576.

Cameron, J. (1982, October). *An early intervention program using temperament characteristics as risk indices.* Presentation at the Biennial Temperament Conference, Salem, MA.

Carey, W. (1972). Clinical applications of infant temperament measures. *Journal of Pediatrics, 81,* 414.

Carey, W. (1982). Clinical use of temperament data in pediatrics. In CIBA Foundation's *Temperamental differences in infants and young children.* London: Pitman.

Carey, W., Fox, M., & McDevitt, S. (1977). Temperament as a factor in early school adjustment. *Pediatrics, 60,* 621-624.

Carey W., & McDevitt, S. (1978). Stability and change in individual temperament diagnoses from infancy to early childhood. *Journal of American Academy of Child Psychiatry, 10,* 331-337.

Carey, W., McDevitt, S., & Baker, J. (1979). Differentiating minimal brain dysfunction and temperament. *Developmental Medicine and Child Neurology, 21,* 765-772.

Cattell, R. B. (1950). *Personality: A systematic and factual study.* New York: McGraw-Hill.

Chamberlin, R. (1981). The relationship of preschool behavior and learning patterns to later school functioning. *Advances in Behavioral Pediatrics, 2,* 111-127.

Clarke-Stewart, A., Umeh, B., Snow, M., & Pederson, J. (1980). Development and prediction of children's sociability from 1 to 2 and 1/2 years. *Developmental Psychology, 16,* 290-302.

Clarke-Stewart, A., VanderStoep, L., & Killian, G. (1979). Analysis and replication of mother-child relations at two years of age. *Child Development, 50,* 777-793.

Clarke-Stewart, A. (1973). Interactions between mothers and their young children: Characteristics and consequences. *Monographs of the Society for Research in Child Development, 38* (Serial No. 153).

Cloninger, C. R., Reich, T., & Yokoyama, S. (1983). Genetic diversity, genome organization, and investigation of the etiology of psychiatric diseases. *Psychiatric Developments, 3,* 225-246.

Coleman, J., Wolkind, S., & Ashley, L. (1977). Symptoms of behaviour disturbance and adjustment to school. *Journal of Child Psychology and Psychiatry, 18,* 201-210.

Daniels, D., Plomin, R., & Greenhalgh, J. (1984). Correlates of difficult temperament in infancy. *Child Development, 55*, 1184-1194.

Denckla, M. (1983). The neuropsychology of social-emotional learning disabilities. *Archives of Neurology, 40*, 461-462.

Dunn, J., & Kendrick, C. (1980). Studying temperament and parent-child interaction: Comparison of interview and direct observation. *Developmental Medicine and Child Neurology, 22*, 484-496.

Earls, F. (1980). The prevalence of behavior problems in three-year-old children: A cross-national replication. *Archives of General Psychiatry, 37*, 1153-1157.

Earls, F. (1981). Temperament characteristics and behavior problems in three-year-old children. *Journal of Nervous and Mental Disorders, 169*, 367-373.

Earls, F., Beardslee, & Garrison. (1987). Correlates and predictors of competence in young children. In E. J. Anthony and B. J. Cohler (Eds.), *The invulnerable child.* New York: Guilford Press.

Earls, F., & Jung, K. G. (in press). Temperament and home environment characteristics as causal factors in the early development of childhood psychopathology. *Journal of the American Academy of Child Psychiatry.*

Emde, R., Gaensbauer, T., & Harmon, R. (1976). Emotional expression in infancy (Monograph). *Psychological Issues, 37.*

Eysenck, H. J., & Eysenck, S.B.G. (1969). *Personality structure and measurement.* London: Routledge & Kegan Paul. Frankel, F., & Simmons, J. (1985). Behavioral treatment approaches to pathological unsocialized physical aggression in young children. *Journal of Child Psychology and Psychiatry, 26*, 525-551.

Freud, S. (1950). Analysis, terminable and interminable. *Collected Papers, 5*, 316-330.

Galambos, N., & Lerner, J. (1987). Child characteristics and the employment of mothers with young children: A longitudinal study. *Journal of Child Psychology and Psychiatry, 28*, 87-98.

Garcia-Coll, C., Kagan, J., & Resnick, S. (1983). Behavioral inhibition in young children. *Child Development, 55*, 1005-1019.

Garmezy, N. (1985). Stress resistant children: The search for protective factors. In J. E. Stevenson (Ed.), *Recent research in developmental psychopathology.* Oxford: Pergamon.

Garrison, W. (1984). Predicting violent behavior in a psychiatric population of boys. *Journal of Youth and Adolescence, 13*, 225-239.

Garrison, W., & Earls, F. (1983). The social context of early human experience. In M. Schmidt & H. Remschmidt (Eds.), *Epidemiology and Child Psychiatry* (Vol. 2). New York: Thieme-Stratton.

Garrison, W., & Earls, F. (1987). Epidemiological perspectives on maternal depression and the young child. In E. Tronick & T. Field (Eds.), *New directions in child development: Maternal and infant depression.* San Francisco: Jossey-Bass.

Garrison, W., & Earls, F. (1984). Change and continuity in child behavior from the preschool period to school entry. In J. Stevenson (Ed.), *Current research in developmental psychopathology* (Book supplement to the *Journal of Child Psychology and Psychiatry*) Oxford: Pergamon Press.

Garrison, W., Earls, F., & Kindlon, D. (1983). An application of the pictorial scale of perceived competence and social acceptance in an epidemiological survey. *Journal of Abnormal Child Psychology, 11*, 367-378.

Garrison, W., Earls, F., & Kindlon, D. (1984). Temperament characteristics in the third year of life and adjustment at school entry. *Journal of Clinical Child Psychology, 13*, 298-303.

Gibbs, M. V., Reeves, D., & Cunningham, C. C. (1987). The application of temperament questionnaires to a British sample: Issues of reliability and validity. *Journal of Child Psychology and Psychiatry, 28*, 61-77.

Goldsmith, H. (1983). Genetic influences on personality from infancy to adulthood. *Child Development, 54*, 331-355.

Goldsmith, H. H., Bradshaw, D. L., & Rieser-Danner, L. A. (19xx). Temperament as a potential developmental influence on attachment. In J. Lerner & R. Lerner (Eds.), *Temperament and social interaction during infancy and childhood*. San Francisco: Jossey-Bass.

Goldsmith, H., Buss, A. H., Plomin, R., Rothbart, M., Thomas, A., Chess, S., Hinde, R., & McCall, R. (1987). Roundtable: What is temperament? *Child Development, 58*, 505-529.

Goldsmith, H., & Campos, J. J. (1982). Toward a theory of infant temperament. In R. Emde & R. Harmon (Eds.), *Attachment and affiliative systems: Neurobiological and psychological aspects*. New York: Plenum.

Goldsmith, H., Duncan, K., & Henderson, C. (1981). *A laboratory-based twin study of infant emotional development*. Paper presented at the annual meetings of the Society for Research in Child Development.

Goldsmith, H., & Gottesman, I. (1981). Origins of variation in behavioral style: A longitudinal study of temperament in young twins. *Child Development, 51*, 91-103.

Graham, P., Rutter, M., & George, S. (1973). Temperamental characteristics as predictors of behavior disorders in children. *American Journal of Orthopsychiatry, 43*, 328-339.

Guilford, J. P. (1959). *Personality*. New York: McGraw-Hill.

Gunn, P., & Berry, P. (1985). The temperament of Down's Syndrome toddlers and their siblings. *Journal of Child Psychology and Psychiatry, 26*, 973-980.

Halverson, C., & Waldrop, M. (1976). Relations between preschool activity and aspects of intellectual and social behavior at 7 and 1/2. *Developmental Psychology, 12*, 107-112.

Hay, D., & Ross, H. (1982). The social nature of early conflict. *Child Development, 53*, 105-113.

Hubert, N., Wachs, T., Peters-Martin, P., & Gandour, M. (1982). The study of early temperament: Measurement and conceptual issues. *Child Development, 53*, 571-600.

Kagan, J. (1966). Reflection-impulsivity: The generality and dynamics of conceptual tempo. *Journal of Abnormal Psychology, 71*, 17-24.

Kagan, J. (1976). Resilience and continuity in psychological development. In A. Clarke and A. Clarke (Eds.), *Early experience: Myth and evidence*. London: Open Books.

Kagan, J. (1982). The construct of difficult temperament: A reply to Thomas, Chess, and Korn. *Merrill-Palmer Quarterly, 28*, 21-24.

Kagan, J. (1982). The emergence of self. *Journal of Child Psychology and Psychiatry, 23*, 363-381.

Kegan, R. (1983). *The evolving self*. Cambridge, MA: Harvard University Press.

Keogh, B. (1982). Children's temperament and teachers' decisions. In CIBA Foundation's *Temperamental differences in infants and young children*. London: Pitman.

Kogan, N. (1976). *Cognitive styles in infancy and early childhood*. Hillsdale, NJ: Lawrence Erlbaum.

Kopp, C. (1982). Antecedents of self-regulation: A developmental perspective. *Developmental Psychology, 18*, 199-214.

Lamb, M. (1980). Unfulfilled promises: A review of *The dynamics of psychological development* by A. Thomas and S. Chess. *Contemporary Psychology, 25*, 906-907.

Lee, M., Vaughn, B., & Kopp, C. (1983). Role of self-control in the performance of very young children on a delayed-response memory-for-location task. *Developmental Psychology, 19*, 40-44.

Lerner, R., Palermo, M., Spiro, A., & Nesselroade, J. (1982). Assessing the dimensions of temperament individuality across the life-span: The Dimensions of Temperament Survey. *Child Development, 53*, 149-159.

Lewis, M., Feiring, C., McGuffog, C., & Jaskir, J. (1984). Predicting psychopathology in six-year-olds from early social relations. *Child Development, 55*, 123-136.

List, K., Sobesky, W., & Braucht, G. (1982, August). *Child-teacher fit and behavior problems in preschool.* Paper presented at the annual meetings of the American Psychological Association, Washington, D.C.

Maccoby, E. E., & Jacklin, C. N. (1974). *The psychology of sex differences.* Palo Alto, CA: Stanford University Press.

Martin, R. (1985). Temperament: A review of research with implications for the school psychologist. *School Psychology Review, 12*, 266-275.

Martin, R. P., Nagle, R., & Paget K. (1985). Relationships between temperament and classroom behavior, teacher attitudes, and academic achievement. *Journal of Psychoeducational Assessment, 1*, 577-586.

Matheny, A. (1980). Bayley's Infant Behavior Record: Behavioral components and twin analyses. *Child Development, 51*, 1157-1167.

Matheny, A., Dolan, A., & Wilson, R. (1976). Twins: Within pair similarity on Bayley's Infant Behavior Record. *Journal of Genetic Psychology, 128*, 263-270.

Matheny, A., & Wilson, R. (1981). Developmental tasks and rating scales for the laboratory assessment of infant temperament. *JSAS Catalog of Selected Documents in Psychology, 11*, 81-82.

Maziade, M., Cote, R., Boutin, P., Bernier, H., & Thivierge, J. (1987). Temperament and intellectual development: A longitudinal study from infancy to four years. *American Journal of Psychiatry, 144*, 144-150.

McDevitt, S. & Carey, W. (1978). The measurement of temperament in 3-7 year old children. *Journal of Child Psychology and Psychiatry, 19*, 245-253.

McDevitt, S., & Carey, W. (1981). Stability of ratings versus perceptions of temperament from early infancy to 1-3 years. *American Journal of Orthopsychiatry, 51*, 342-345.

Mead, G. H. (1934). *Mind, self, and society.* Chicago: University of Chicago Press.

Mellsop, G. W. (1972). Psychiatric patients seen as children and adults: Childhood predictors of adult illness. *Journal of Child Psychology and Psychiatry, 13*, 91-101.

Messer, S. (1976). Reflection-impulsivity: A review. *Psychological Bulletin, 83*, 1026-1052.

Monahan, J. (1984). The prediction of violent behavior: Toward a second generation of theory and policy. *American Journal of Psychiatry, 141*, 10-15.

O'Leary, K. (1980). Pills or skills for hyperactive children. *Journal of Applied Behavior Analysis, 13*, 191-204.

Olweus, D. (1979). Stability of aggressive reaction patterns in males: A review. *Psychological Bulletin, 86*, 852-875.

Pasaminick, B., & Knobloch, H. (1966). Retrospective studies on the epidemiology of reproductive casualty: Old and new. *Merrill-Palmer Quarterly, 12*, 7-26.

Patterson, G. (1975). The aggressive child: Victim and architect of a coercive system. In L. Hamerlynk, L. Handy, & E. Mash (Eds.), *Behavior modification and families*. New York: Brunner/Mazel.

Pavlov, I. P. (1927). *Conditioned reflexes: An investigation of the physiological activity of the cerebral cortex* (Ed. and Trans., G. V. Anrep). London: Oxford University Press.

Pavlov, I. (1955). *General types of animal and human nervous activity*. Moscow: Foreign Language Publishing House.

Persson-Blennow, I. & McNeil, T. (1979). A questionnaire for measurement of temperament in six-month-old infants: Development and standardization. *Journal of Child Psychology and Psychiatry, 20*, 1-13.

Plomin, R. (1976). Extraversion: Sociability and impulsivity. *Journal of Personality Assessment, 40*, 24-30.

Plomin, R. (1982). Childhood temperament. In B. Lahey & A. Kazdin (Eds.), *Advances in clinical child psychology*(Vol. 6, pp. 2-80). New York: Plenum.

Plomin, R., & Daniels, D. (1984). Genetics and shyness. In W. Jones, J. Cheek, & S. Briggs (Eds.), *A sourcebook on shyness: Research and treatment. New York: Plenum.

Plomin, R., & DeFries, J. (1985). Origins of individual differences in infancy. Orlando, FL: Academic Press.

Plomin, R., & Dunn, J. (1986). *The study of early temperament: Changes, continuities, and challenges*. Hillsdale, New Jersey: Erlbaum.

Plomin, R., & Rowe, D. C. (1977). A twin study of temperament in young children. *Journal of Psychology, 97*, 107-113.

Rappoport, J., Pandoni, C., Renfield, M., Lake, C., & Ziegler, M. (1977). Newborn dopamine-B-hydroxylase, minor physical anomalies, and infant temperament. *American Journal of Psychiatry, 134*, 676-679.

Richman, N., Graham, P., & Stevenson, J. (1982). *Preschool to school: A behavioral study*. London: Academic Press.

Robins, L. (1966). *Deviant children grown up*. Baltimore, MD: Williams and Wilkins.

Rothbart, M. (1981). Measurement of temperament in infancy. *Child Development, 52*, 569-578.

Rothbart, M., & Derryberry, D. (1981). Development of individual differences in temperament. In M. Lamb & A. Brown (Eds.), *Advances in developmental psychology* (Vol. 1). Hillsdale, NJ: Lawrence Erlbaum.

Rutter, M. (1980). DSM-III: A step forward or back in terms of the classification of child psychiatric disorders? *Journal of American Academy of Child Psychiatry, 19*, 371-394.

Rutter, M. (1981). Stress, coping and development: Some issues and some questions. *Journal of Child Psychology and Psychiatry, 22*, 323-356.

Rutter, M. (1982). Temperament: Concepts, issues and problems. In CIBA Foundation's *Temperamental differences in infants and young children*. London: Pitman.

Rutter, M. (1983). *Developmental Neuropsychiatry*. New York: Guilford.

Sameroff, A. (1978). Summary and conclusions: The future of newborn assessment. In A. Sameroff (Ed.), Organization and stability of newborn behavior: A commentary on the Brazelton Neonatal Behavior Scale. *Monographs of the Society of Research in Child Development, 43*, 102-117.

Scarr, S., & McCartney, K. (1983). How people make their own environments: A theory of genotype-environment effects. *Child Development, 54*, 424-435.

Scholom, A., & Schiff, G. (1980). Relating infant temperament to learning disabilities. *Journal of Abnormal Child Psychology, 8*, 127-132.

Scholom, A., Zucker, R., & Stollak, G. (1979). Relating early child adjustment to infant and parent temperament. *Journal of Abnormal Child Psychology, 17*, 297-303.

Selman, R. L. (1980). *The growth of interpersonal understanding.* New York: Academic Press.

Sheldon, W. (1942). *The varieties of temperament: A psychology of constitutional differences.* New York: Harper & Row.

Sjobring, H. (1973). Personality structure and development: A model and its applications. *Acta Psychiatrica Scandinavica, 244,* (Suppl.).

Sobesky, W., Braucht, G., & List, K. (1984, August). *Stability of child-teacher fit: A longitudinal study.* Paper presented at the annual meeting of the American Psychological Association, Toronto.

Sobesky, W., List, K., Holden, D., & Braucht, N. (1981). *Dimensions of child temperament in school settings.* Paper presented at the biennial meeting of the Society for Research in Child Development, Boston.

Spitz, R. (1965). *The first year of life.* New York: International Universities Press.

Sroufe, L. A. (1985). Attachment classification from the perspective of the infant-caregiver relationships and infant temperament. *Child Development, 56,* 1-14.

Strelau, J. (1969). *Temperament and the type of nervous system.* Warsaw: PWN.

Super, C. M. (1976). Environmental effects on motor development in Kenya. *Developmental Medicine and Child Neurology, 18,* 561-567.

Terestman, N. (1980). Mood quality and intensity in nursery school children as predictors of behavior disorders. *American Journal of Orthopsychiatry, 50,* 125-128.

Thomas, A., & Chess, S. (1977). *Temperament and development.* New York: Brunner/Mazel.

Thomas, A., & Chess, S. (1984). Genesis and evolution of behavioral disorder: From infancy to early adult life. *American Journal of Psychiatry, 141,* 1-9.

Thomas, A., Chess, S., & Birch, H. G. (1968). *Temperament and behavior disorders in children.* New York: New York University Press.

Thomas, A., Chess, S., Birch, H., Hertzig, M., & Korn, S. (1963). *Behavioral individuality in early childhood.* New York: New York University Press.

Thomas, A., Chess, S., & Korn, S. (1982). The reality of difficult temperament. *Merrill-Palmer Quarterly, 28,* 1-20.

Tronick, E. (1987). *New directions in child development: Maternal and infant depression.*

Tronick, E., Ricks, M., & Cohn, J. (1982). Maternal and infant affective exchange: Patterns of adaptation. In T. Field & A. Fogel (Eds.), *Emotion and early interaction.* Hillsdale, NJ: Lawrence Erlbaum.

Watson, J. B. (1924). *Behaviorism.* New York: W.W. Norton.

Weber, R. A., Levitt, M. J., & Clark, M. C. (1986). Individual variation in attachment security and strange situation behavior: The role of maternal and infant temperament. *Child Development, 57,* 56-65.

Webster-Stratton, C., & Eyberg, S. (1982). Child temperament: Relationship with child behavior problems and parent-child interactions. *Journal of Clinical Child Psychology, 11,* 123-129.

Weissbluth, M. (1981). Sleep duration and infant temperament. *Journal of Pediatrics, 99,* 817-819.

Weissbluth, M. (1982). Sleep apnea, sleep duration, and infant temperament. *Journal of Pediatrics, 101,* 307-310.

Weissbluth, M. et al. (1983). Signs of airway obstruction during sleep and behavioral, developmental and academic problems. *Developmental and Behavioral Pediatrics, 4*, 119-121.

Weissbluth, M., & Green, O. (1983). Plasma progesterone concentrations in infants: Relation to infant colic. *Journal of Pediatrics, 103*, 935-936.

Weintraub, S., & Mesulam, M. (1983). Developmental learning disabilities of the right hemisphere: Emotional, interpersonal, and cognitive components. *Archives of Neurology, 40*, 463-468.

Wenar, C. (1982). Developmental psychopathology: Its nature and models. *Journal of Clinical Child Psychology, 11*, 192-201.

Werner, H., & Kaplan, B. (1963). *Symbol formation: An organismic-developmental approach to language and the expression of thought.* New York: John Wiley.

Wilson, R. S., & Matheny, A. P. (1983). Assessment of temperament in infant twins. *Developmental Psychology, 19*, 172-183.

Wirt, R., Lachar, D., Klinedinst, J., & Seat, P. (1981). *Multidimensional description of child personality: A manual for the Personality Inventory for Children.* Los Angeles: Western Psychological Services.

Wolfson, J., Fields, J. H., & Rose, S. (1987). Symptoms, temperament resiliency, and control in anxiety-disordered preschool children. *Journal of the American Academy of Child Psychiatry, 26*, 16-22.

Worobey, J. (1986). Convergence among assessments of temperament in the first month. *Child Development, 57*, 47-55.

Zimbardo, P. (1977) *Shyness.* Reading, PA: Addison- Wesley.

AUTHOR INDEX

SUBJECT INDEX

Activity level   23, 27, 33-36, 40, 44-45, 47, 51, 54, 58, 70, 74-75, 86
Adaptability   33-34, 47, 51, 54, 59
Affect   36, 38, 42, 89
Aggression   23, 27, 69, 74, 76
Anxiety   93
Approach/withdrawal   34, 39, 47, 64, 74
Assessment   35-38, 42-49, 51-52, 54-56, 61, 77, 86, 90-91; clinical, 66-69, 92-93
Attachment   83
Attention Deficit Disorder with Hyperactivity   54, 70-74
Attention span   36, 47, 51, 54

Behavior problems   53-55, 58, 62, 69, 72-79; continuity of   60, 63, 88; prediction of   55-56, 60, 63-64, 77, 82-83
Behavioral style   32-34, 47, 73, 79, 86, 89

Child Behavior Profile   60
Chromosomic aberrations   23-26
Clinical application   66-69, 72-81, 83, 92-93; in pediatric setting   67
Cognition   36, 37, 40, 42, 89
Colorado Adoption Project   82, 91, 95
Colorado Childhood Temperament Inventory   45
Constellation analyses   51-52
Continuity, contextual   36, 45, 53, 55, 58, 88-89
Continuity, temporal   14, 31, 34-36, 39, 41, 47-49, 52-53, 58, 64-65, 70, 88-89, 91-92
Cooperativeness   36
Cross-sectional research   53-55
Crying   33

Definitional issues   11-12, 15, 31, 42, 85, 87-89, 95

Development in childhood   39, 41, 88-89, 92, 95; and behavior problems   69, 85
Development, lifespan   47
Difficult child   33, 51-52, 56, 69, 93
Dimensional analyses   21, 32-35, 44, 46-47, 52, 58, 75
Dimensions of Temperament Survey   47, 67, 90
Distractibility   34, 37
Distress to limitations   44

EASI   35, 42, 51
Easy child   33, 52
Emotional development   39, 92
Emotional lability   92
Emotional tone   36
Emotionality   35, 45, 86, 92
Environmental influences   40-41, 44, 52, 60, 65; and genetic influences   14-15, 29, 32, 91
Evolutionary theory   22, 29

Family disturbance   53, 60
Fastidiousness of behavior   56
Fearfulness   39, 44, 60, 64, 92-93
Feeding   33
Fixation   92

Genetic Field Theory   39
Genetic influences   12-13, 21, 23-26, 29-30, 35-36, 42, 82, 86, 95; and environmental influences   14-15, 28-29, 32, 91, 95; and neurophysiology   20, 23; population studies   27-28; and psychopathology   26; and sex differences   23; twin studies   27, 36
Goodness of fit   38, 41, 47, 49, 52, 57-58, 62, 68, 73-74, 83; assessment of   67

ABOUT THE AUTHORS

William T. Garrison is Director of Pediatric Research at the Baystate Medical Center in Springfield, Massachusetts, and Associate Professor of Pediatrics at the University of Massachusetts Medical School. He received a doctorate in Psychology at Cornell University and pursued postdoctoral specialty training in Clinical Child Psychology at the Harvard Medical School and the McLean Hospital. He has been on the faculty of the Harvard Medical School, the Washington University School of Medicine, and has been on staff at the McLean Hospital, the Boston Children's Hospital Medical Center, and the St. Louis Children's Hospital. His research interests primarily involve the etiology and classification of early childhood disorders, child/adolescent aggression and violence, and mental health services for children in primary health-care settings.

Felton J. Earls is Blanche F. Ittleson Professor of Child Psychiatry and Director of the William Greenleaf Eliot Division of Child Psychiatry at Washington University School of Medicine. He received his M.D. from Howard University, and trained in general psychiatry at the Massachusetts General Hospital and child psychiatry at Boston Children's Hospital Medical Center. Prior to coming to Washington University he was on the faculty of the Harvard Medical School. His research contributions have been devoted to the application of epidemiologic approaches to the study of early childhood psychopathology.

NOTES